Talent Mindset

The Business Owner's Guide to Building Bench Strength

By Stacy Feiner, PsyD

with
Kristen Hampshire

Feiner Consulting, LLC
Cleveland, Ohio

Editor and writing collaborator: Kristen Hampshire

Copy editor & book design: Randy Wood

Cover design: Arlene Watson

Photography: Stacy Marinelli

Author's photo: Jerry Mann

Published by: Feiner Consulting, LLC
ISBN: 978-0-9908664-0-4
Library of Congress Control Number: 2014914318

Printed in the USA at Color House Graphics, Grand Rapids, MI

Praise for Talent Mindset

"Business success is all about having the right talent and getting them to pull together in the right direction. Talent Mindset *speaks truthfully and directly to middle-market business owners with a step-by-step guide for accomplishing this. Feiner's advice is compelling. Don't wait. Read this book and get moving."*

—David Pottruck
Best-selling author of *Stacking the Deck: How to Lead Breakthrough Change Against Any Odds*

*"*Talent Mindset *offers a powerful framework that bookends the critical drivers of talent management rightfully between strategy and culture. It belongs in the hands of business leaders who believe that people at all levels of the organization are the means for creating sustainable prosperity. And, in the hands of HR managers, who are in the position to facilitate effective talent-management. Resounding and memorable."*

—Robert Widing
Dean of the Weatherhead School of Management at Case Western Reserve University

"Stacy has created a thoughtful and strategic approach to talent management, one of the most critical and foundational systems in an organization. Talent Mindset *is an accessible, step-by-step guide that gives business owners all of the tools to engage the talent in their organizations."*

—Jodi Berg
President and CEO, Vitamix Corporation

"*In today's economy, we need to make every day and every employee count.* Talent Mindset *focuses us on how to be successful leading people, while untangling us from all of the misconceptions and failed attempts of the past.*"

—A. Ray Dalton
Founder and president, Dalton Foundation

"Talent Mindset *is the de facto playbook for getting your arms around the job of leading people. Middle-market business owners and senior management teams finally have a how-to guide for building a bench that is the company's ultimate competitive advantage.*"

—John M. Deignan
President, Americhem

"Talent Mindset *gives owners the thought process and tools to build bench strength within their organization. Stacy provides a straightforward framework that can be adapted to any business at any stage of talent development.*"

—Rachel Wallis-Andreasson
Executive vice president, Wallis Companies

To My Bench...

Happiness is found in the garden of gratitude.

Thank you to those who brought enthusiasm, love and friendship to my book journey. Thank you for staying curious about my progress, celebrating mini milestones, and seeing this endeavor as a natural outgrowth for me.

Worry is a waste of imagination.

Thank you to those who brought me expertise—whose experience and wisdom helped me trust my work, convey my ideas and reach a larger audience.

Self-awareness is your greatest competitive advantage.

Thank you to my clients and readers who are restless to find new insights and willing to dig deep within themselves to perform better today than yesterday. I admire how you strive to reach your potential and help others do the same.

Special thanks to:

My parents, who gave me my first guitar and encouraged me to sing my own songs. Ruth Chad, who was my first model for great coaching. Kristen Hampshire, who collaborated with me to write this book. And my husband, Peter McCarren, whose beautiful way of seeing the world broadens my way of seeing the world...and for our two beautiful children.

Contents

Foreword

As I read Talent Mindset, I experienced a replay of many discoveries made while working with Stacy as my coach. My business is in its fourth generation of family leadership. I knew my great grandfather who came to the office to witness the company's progress until his death in his nineties. His quirks and passions are still imprinted on the business, 75 years after he created it. With Stacy's help, my team is aspiring to leverage the good things that are born from this evolution, namely trust, stewardship and integrity. At the same time, we see that we must bring out the latent boldness and ambition that are often subdued or abandoned in lieu of safety and conservatism, things that served the business well through challenges and change.

Having a business in your blood, the challenge can be in feeling worthy of big aspirations like deliberate growth, performance and talent that are thought to be found only in larger, more recognizable firms. The draw of Talent Mindset is that it speaks to an immensely under-served audience— the owners of middle-market businesses, who are often overlooked by the legions of business authors who seek to reach a larger audience by touting the successes or failures of mega corporations. Our unsung battles are more unique, complex and seemingly microscopic at times.

Middle-market businesses are anything but generic. They are, in fact, organic. Therefore, knowingly or not, we lead with an organic sense of leadership that is closer to the source of value-creation and deserves a different approach. We don't need to, and indeed we should not, compare ourselves to mega corporations. We haven't traded entrepreneurialism for bureaucracy. Our leadership is based on personal choices, not a corporate formula. Talent Mindset is about reviving business owners' belief in themselves. It awakens us. And when applied, it empowers us.

Talent Mindset is a framework that is flexible, yet strictly values-based and, as such, is a real innovation. Having arrived in a position of leadership somewhat by virtue of genetics, leaders of family businesses are humble about their influence on the enterprise. Stacy's mantra of enhancing self-awareness, instilling a philosophy, implementing a sound system and ultimately building a strong bench are things we can all do. Stacy prods us to realize that we can be and must be great.

Michael Forde Ripich
President and CEO, AT&F Co.

Getting Into the Talent Mindset

Knowing your talent is as important as knowing your numbers.

The people you surround yourself with in your organization make or break your success. No one succeeds alone. The individuals you hire, promote and entrust with critical information—the professionals you expect to execute your company mission—are your greatest competitive advantage, or the biggest drag. They're the champions for your company or a substantial drain on time, money, resources and potential.

When engaged, leveraged and optimized, your talent will drive your organization to be agile, innovative, profitable, smart—successful. Your success or failure depends upon the people you allow into your company.

So many times, business owners recruit and develop leaders without realizing that their hiring and development choices are random, impulsive, disjointed and disconnected to their objectives and strategies. Their choices are not adding value. Their people are, more or less, hastily drafted into the organization through a borrowed hiring process, never truly onboarded, and then neglected in terms of performance management and development. It's no wonder so many employees and leaders feel disengaged, uninspired and checked out.

Stop for a moment and consider the people in your organization. Do you remember why you hired that vice president of sales or of operations? What made you think that controller was the best person for the job? Was it convenience—his application hit your desk when you had a hole to fill? How did your senior team get to where they are today? Were they promoted? Hired from the outside? Why this and not that person? What skills does each individual bring to the organization that makes him or her a valuable player? What characteristics make each a cultural fit for your company?

If you feel stumped, you're not alone. We surround ourselves with people. But why do we feel, in so many instances, like we are stuck with what we have, that we are carrying dead weight or that we do not have the right "fit" for an important leadership position? As an owner, you might be thinking, "How did I let this happen? Can I turn this around?"

Yes. What you need is a working knowledge of your talent inventory across your enterprise. A working knowledge of your talent allows you to align it to the greater strategy. Businesses need good people. And as an owner, you must have a working knowledge of your talent bench.

This book is your field guide to Strategic Talent Management, a platform with nine Centers of Excellence that will help you analyze, understand and implement organizational improvements surrounding your people. Strategic Talent Management puts you in the ready position to enhance value, optimize talent, prepare for growth, posture for sale, or transition to the next generation.

Strategic Talent Management gives you the know-how, intelligence and control to leverage your people. You can recruit top talent, train and develop the best players, and ready your talent for new challenges. It gives you agility to deploy top talent. By working this system, you can lead your company toward peak performance.

With the right mindset and people on your team, and the right equipment (talent management) to steer them toward a win, the only variables should be external conditions. Strategic Talent Management prepares you for those X-factors because you'll have the team in place to compete in any environment.

When an organization prioritizes Strategic Talent Management, builds bench strength and goes to market with a high-performing team, it will:

- Increase profitability
- Attract top talent
- Create an environment for people to do their best work
- Bring value to the community
- Broaden transition options: keep the wealth engine in the family or owned by the employees
- Realize that its leadership philosophy is powerful and execute it successfully

How Strategic Talent Management Works

With Strategic Talent Management, you start where you are and address your greatest "people pain." Many owners begin this journey by identifying a single problem (such as recruiting), then a trend is spotted: Perhaps the business repeatedly recruits and hires people who fail the organization after six months.

Working through the nine Centers of Excellence, you'll prioritize what competencies require the greatest attention immediately. Then, you'll work through the Strategic Talent Management continuum. The framework is fundamental, while the processes are designed to suit your company's human capital needs; and you'll draw from the framework provided in this book to support a new way of thinking about Strategic Talent Management in your company.

There might be pieces-parts of the talent management continuum already in place at your organization you can rely on. But there will be holes. Those gaps are where errors in hiring and the way we deal with people altogether can occur.

Here is how the Strategic Talent Management framework is organized:

Strategy and culture: These bookend Strategic Talent Management so that your people are intrinsically connected to your drivers for success.

Corridors: These are the three key components for creating a talent infrastructure for your company. You can think of the Corridors as "levels" of the process, and they align with the lifecycle of your talent. The Strategic Talent Management Corridors are: Talent Acquisition, Talent Development and Talent Deployment.

Centers of Excellence: The nine centers are steps that connect the Corridors. To successfully establish each Corridor, you will work through three Centers of Excellence that help you fully develop an aspect of your talent management. The Nine Centers of Excellence are: Recruiting, Selection, Onboarding, Training, Performance Management,

Leadership Development, Talent Inventory, Succession and Employee Engagement.

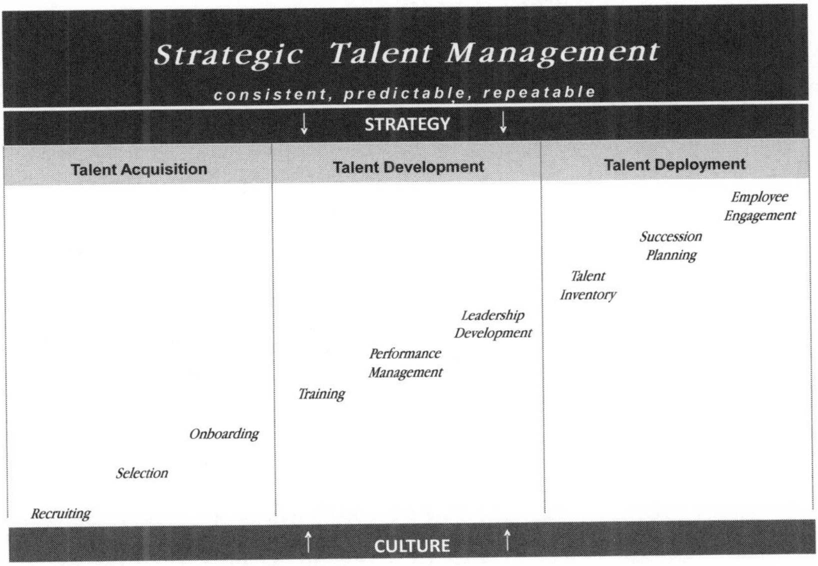

Figure 1: Strategic Talent Management provides the infrastructure that bridges your strategy to your culture. The system builds bench strength, giving your business the agility to face transitions and achieve goals. Ultimately, Strategic Talent Management is the intersection of culture, leadership, talent and succession.

The Corridors and Centers of Excellence

The three Strategic Talent Management Corridors form a basis for who you hire (Acquisition), how you develop them (Development), and why you advance them (Deployment). This book is divided by Corridors: Talent Acquisition, Talent Development and Talent Deployment. Each chapter within those Corridors covers the Centers of Excellence. As you operationalize each Center of Excellence that falls within these Corridors, you will build a more aligned organization where your people and business objectives work as one.

17

Talent Acquisition:
- *Recruiting*: Filling your company's pipeline with talented, qualified candidates
- *Selection*: Putting in place a rigorous, progressive, sequenced process of teasing out top talent to place in your organization
- *Onboarding*: Setting the tone for new hires and assimilating them into the culture providing direction and resources; reviving the team's commitment to success

Talent Development:
- *Training*: Creating a culture of continuous learning, curiosity, innovation and discovery
- *Performance management*: Designing a system of accountability for career conversations that help managers and employees understand what it takes to succeed, and how success is measured and rewarded
- *Leadership development*: Developing high performers and improving productivity to fund the future of your company

Talent Deployment:
- *Talent inventory*: Evaluating talent across the enterprise, creating a talent slate, and engineering a plan to align, stretch and deploy talent
- *Succession*: Building bench strength across the organization, preparing for transitions and transferring institutional knowledge
- *Employee engagement:* Getting to the crux of a company's culture

Working The System

Strategic Talent Management is different than other systems because you can "hop on" at any Corridor, and begin with any Center of Excellence. You determine where on the wheel to start your journey based on your greatest people pains.

You can read this book from beginning to end, or skip to the chapter that best applies to your business's human-capital concerns right now. Eventually, you'll work your way through the continuum because the quality of the data that comes from each Corridor fuels and propels the next Corridor. Over time, the Strategic Talent Management becomes embedded into your culture. It changes the way you think, manage and plan for the future. It changes the way you lead.

Along with providing a framework and philosophy, we'll share stories from the front lines of implementing Strategic Talent Management, and Talent Insight notes so you can begin your journey today.

Figure 2: Are you ahead of the conversation?

Start With the People Pain

In my Strategic Talent Management practice, most clients come to me because they want to confront a specific problem related to the way they hire, train, develop, promote or otherwise manage their people. There's usually one thing, a sore spot that drives the owner to seek coaching for improvement. That's the seed, where we start to address Strategic Talent Management. From there, the process unfolds.

Here are three business scenarios that present common people pains, and which Corridor to start your journey on the Strategic Talent Management continuum based on each challenge.

Scenario 1—Talent Acquisition: A new person you enthusiastically hired with high expectations for performance has failed, again. Your recruiting process can't seem to weed out the winners from the losers. And worse yet, when you can't find the qualified candidates to fill your need, you hang on to dead weight and are forced to keep swimming against the tide.

Figure 3: Talent Acquisition starting point

Scenario 2—Talent Development: You don't see any glaring problems with the way your company is operating, but you worry it is stagnant, in a rut. Your company was humming along, but now it feels like it's plodding. Your team is running on autopilot. Everyone is status quo. Employee turnover is rare—the leadership team has tenure. The business is not suffering in the sense that you're constantly putting out fires but things aren't right. You can't really put a finger on a specific problem, and you fall into an, "If it ain't broke, don't fix it," mentality. You find yourself playing not to lose. Everyone is focused on today. Nothing is wrong with the people and you can't claim failure. But you are not reaching long-term objectives and the organization feels stagnant.

You want to peak perform and you are looking for something more: growth, revenue, new products, expansion, ambitious managers, engaged workers, innovation, energy, accountability, the list goes on.

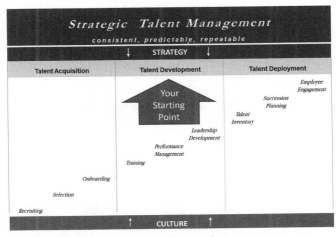

Figure 4: Talent Development starting point

Scenario 3—Talent Deployment: You feel stuck between a rock and a hard place: you can't find the talent inside the company that'll get you to the next level, but trying to hire from the outside seems useless too. You wonder if your top managers are holding back the next tier of leaders because they've become over reliant on them. There is no pipeline of talent—no bench of future leaders in the waiting.

The company is at great risk because of its lack of talent reserves. Meanwhile, when your managers do come together to evaluate their people, they are all over the map. Some managers overrate their people to make themselves look good, and others underrate their people as a way to keep everyone on their toes. Your leaders are not using a shared set of criteria to discuss their people. These inconsistencies inhibit honest discussions of talent and create barriers in the boardroom. Because there is no set of shared criteria, making accurate performance evaluations is difficult—and even more complicated is making decisions about promotions and succession.

You want to build a bench of strong, talented individuals to take the company into the future, but there is no enterprise-wide system in place for doing so.

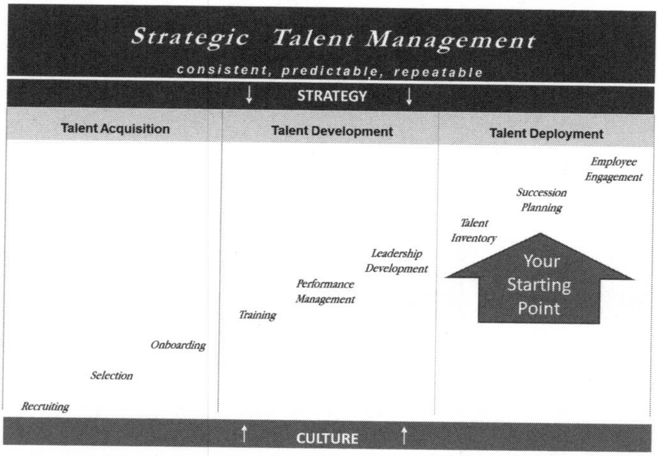

Figure 5: Talent Deployment starting point

Implementing Strategic Talent Management

Strategic Talent Management gives you a working knowledge of your people so you can move, retool, reassign and deploy. You can flex because your people can. What would your life be like if you had an agile organization that allowed you to rapidly execute business decisions? Strategic Talent Management increases your awareness of the people who work in your company, and the people you hire. This inevitably deepens your understanding of the capabilities of your business.

But how long does it take to implement this process, exactly? Effective talent management is a long-term commitment that generally involves a minimum of 18 months to design and up to three years to embed into the culture. Then, it requires ongoing refinement. Strategic Talent Management is the difference between what you want now, and what you want the most.

No business can afford to put this talent imperative on the back burner. When a business operates with a talent turnstile, the cost is staggering—a painful drain of resources and an unrecoverable loss of time. No operation can afford to hire the wrong people and absorb inadequate performance, despite the fact that business owners pay out the nose anyway.

Consider this: If you hire an employee whose salary is $40,000, and they turn out to be an underperformer, your recruiting cost is an estimated $400,000. That includes filling the pipeline, screening the pool and hiring the candidate to training, development, morale and lost opportunity endeavor. That's ten times the person's salary in the first year.

You may realize as soon as 90 days that the individual is not a fit—that he or she slipped through the cracks—or as late as 18 months. By then it's too late to recover your investment. You're in the red with this hire, and continued employment of an individual who is not serving your company's strategic goals affects productivity, profitability and morale.

Strategic Talent Management seals these cracks.

Now, do the math and consider the number of people you have recruited and hired in the past three to five years only to discover a staggering number of misfires.

In contrast, a high-functioning business where Strategic Talent Management is at work operates with an ideal 70 to 30 ratio: internal candidates fill 70 percent of open positions and 30 percent go to new-hires from outside the organization. How does your organization compare to this benchmark?

Owning the Process:
Your Talent, Your Strategy

In many ways, Strategic Talent Management is like parenting a child. Your business is a living organism that needs parenting. It's a living, breathing community of people that needs to be nurtured by the person who wants it most to perform well, which is you, the business owner. When a leader neglects to proactively design Strategic Talent Management, the company by default becomes a reflection of his or her idiosyncrasies—the worst habits of its owner.

The Strategic Talent Management philosophy we provide here begins with you, the owner. You steer the process. You become a student of how to acquire, develop and deploy talent. This story is about developing a system to usher in the type of people you've been dreaming of—the people you deserve to have working with you. And, it's about finding freedom as an owner through proper talent placement, and about gaining a competitive edge because of the human capital driving your organization. This story is about turning a "stuck" business into a highly networked, engaged business that offers a rich, rewarding environment where people can contribute at their highest level and thrive. It's powerful. It's about winning. You are the hero of the story.

25

Reality Check: Where Do You Stand?

Strategic Talent Management must be a customized process that is every bit as personal as your company's vision. Ultimately, Strategic Talent Management is your vision. You own it. First, you have to get a grasp on what it means to your organization and how you can usher in this forward-thinking plan. That's what we'll spend time doing in this book.

So, where does your company stand in terms of talent, and in general? Before you get started with the Strategic Talent Management process, take a bit of time to consider what challenges are impeding your organization's success and your achievement as a leader? In your business, what old ways of thinking are tethering you to old systems, to traditional ways of operating—and the same old results, steady (but not stellar) performance?

As you become more self-aware and open to what's truly happening in your business today, you'll have a greater ability to:

- See your people as a system, a community of people there to join you on a mission
- Allow talent to surface
- Understand how talent matters to your organization
- Deploy and leverage talent across the enterprise
- Create an environment where rigorous thinking and conversations unearth bold solutions
- Establish a culture where honest exchanges of ideas are viewed as a privilege and responsibility
- Evolve the organization at the speed of your talent
- Be decisive as a leader, and take extreme action

The Strategic Talent Management process is not complicated, but it does require sweat equity—your sweat equity as the owner. You will need to fully commit to Strategic Talent Management and invest in the vision. In doing so, it will revitalize you as a leader. You will be challenged to think differently about yourself, your people and the way you do things today. You will feel uncomfortable at times and forced to face with a strange phenomenon—why you have not done what you keep saying you want to do. You will look at data that you already have in your organization and use it differently. You will unearth new data, which will lead to new ways of thinking. You will learn how to transform information into valuable intelligence.

Data generated in one Center of Excellence directly applies to the other eight centers. Each center builds on the next and is a valuable component to the whole system. You will extract better intelligence, use it for rigorous discussions, apply it for better decisions and execute with buy-in.

Figure 6: Strategic Talent Management is a cyclical and ongoing process where each center builds on the next.

Gaining Self-Awareness: Strategic Talent Management Starts With You

The Strategic Talent Management process starts with one person, the owner, before the process is launched as a company-wide initiative. Before you begin reshaping the talent at your organization, start by looking carefully at your own leadership practices. What are you doing to create an environment where people can do their best work? You have the power to change the way your business operates and "acts." You can lament about how the local or federal government isn't paving the way for your business to succeed—that regulations or the economy or politics in general are a block to your success. But I urge you to take stock of how well you are leading as the president of your own "country"—your company. If you want your people to peak perform, you must peak perform.

Self-awareness is a critical first step to launching Strategic Talent Management—we're talking about the capacity to acknowledge your impact and influence on others and the environment. This requires honestly assessing your own performance, commitment to greatness and willingness to do the work required to get there. You must recognize the innumerable choices available to help you engage your people and your environment; and you must act with integrity, compassion and a drive to peak perform. This level of self-awareness will give you the mindset to implement a drastically different way of recruiting, developing and engaging your people. (You don't have to go it alone. You just have to commit to doing it right.)

At the end of the day, self-awareness is a leader's ultimate competitive advantage. As a leader, your ability to steer the organization through transitions impacts your ability to thrive and win. Self-awareness for a leader is critical because to maximize your company's potential, your leadership skills must evolve at the same pace that your business is growing. When the pace of change is fast and you're hunkered down focused on the day-to-day, you can miss transitions and quickly fall short as the business moves forward. Self-awareness is about recognizing that with every business stage, you'll confront new complexities. Understanding what the company needs from you as its leader, will propel growth. You'll be in tune with your business, your people and what the future holds. Combine an acute level of self-awareness with talent—and the ability to acquire, develop and deploy your people—and you'll have the vision and strategy to win in any economic environment, under any circumstances.

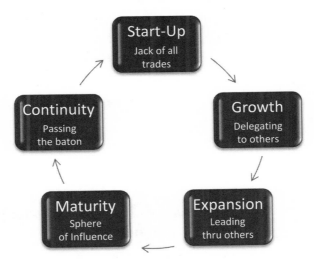

Figure 7: The Leadership lifecycle. As a business evolves, the owner must evolve as a leader. New leadership competencies and honest self-analysis are the keys to keeping pace with the business's growing needs. Business owners can lose sight of these five predictable transition points, causing leadership to lag behind the needs of the business. The lesson: Keep pace so you can advance the goals of the company rather than unintentionally holding it back.

Play to Win: A Coach, A Confidante

Developing the self-awareness to initiate radical change, create systems like Strategic Talent Management, and direct a strategic vision is not something you do alone. Every elite athlete works with a coach. Ambitious business leaders should, too. As you work through this Strategic Talent Management process, you might consider drafting an informal board of advisors as a sounding board. And, enlist in a coach you trust to help you execute the nine Centers of Excellence. It's true that no one knows your business better than you. You own it. But because you are entrenched in the operation—it is so much a part of you that you eat, sleep, breathe and bleed it—you need new, insights, constructive advice so you can see what you should do differently (and better) so you can lead your business to what's next. You need advising to keep you alert, honest about yourself, and to open your eyes to new ideas. (It's easy to get stuck in your own thinking when ideas are not challenged.) And, so you can advance your business goals in any economic environment.

I relate this to the way elite performers have an innate restlessness that continuously pushes them to achieve at their highest level. Sometimes their trajectory is clear and coaching is about fine-tuning. Other times, elite performers have goals for themselves and their company that they just aren't reaching and coaching is about digging deep.

You set high standards for your business, and you should set even higher standards for yourself. During the Strategic Talent Management process, there will be a necessary tension that surfaces when you work through talent challenges. This tension will spur discovery. There should be uncomfortable conversations—awkward silences from time to time. There should be brave thinking. And, ultimately, results you can measure.

As you gain self-awareness, you'll build a leadership mindset to launch Strategic Talent Management. In the following chapters, you'll learn the Strategic Talent Management system and how to engineer it to reflect your philosophy and the aspirations you can now articulate because of your coaching experiences. You become the master of the process at your company. We'll walk you through that thinking in this book. Finally, through continued coaching, you will continue to influence, grow, evolve and drive forward. You will be compelled by purpose and profitability. You'll build the bench strength required to compete in the new economy.

Now is the time to change the way you acquire, develop and engage people. *Talent Mindset: A Business Owner's Guide to Building Bench Strength* provides a fresh framework for executing Strategic Talent Management, and a philosophy to help you understand why it matters. This is your field guide for turning talent into your company's greatest asset—so dog-ear the pages, break the spine, use your highlighter. Enlist your team in the process. It is a cooperative effort. Eventually, you will customize your own talent management processes that leverage the framework of the Centers of Excellence infrastructure.

Corridor:
Acquisition

On the Strategic Talent Management continuum, the Acquisition Centers of Excellence (Recruiting, Selection, Onboarding) focus on bringing high-performing individuals into the fold, carefully vetting candidates by creating meaningful interview experiences, and optimizing efficiency when integrating new hires into the culture. Recruiting is about filling the pipeline of qualified candidates with a network-driven plan and bench-strength building mindset. Selection focuses on thoughtfully and scientifically evaluating candidates; and Onboarding is when new hires are effectively integrated into the culture so they can adopt a sense of ownership in the organization's vision.

Recruiting:
A Mission-Focused Approach

Talent Acquisition is one part candidate and ten parts company, which means the majority of the process is completely in your control. This is great news because if you're doing recruiting well, it's to your credit. And if it isn't going well, you have the control to fix it. But the reality is, there is serious risk involved in recruiting, and the process should be much more rigorous than most companies expect.

Recruiting involves putting together a hiring committee, coming to consensus on hiring criteria, screening applicants, and filling your company's pipeline with qualified candidates. Recruiting is the launch pad to effective Strategic Talent Acquisition—next comes Selection then Onboarding. Recruiting is complicated because, in addition to filling the pipeline and qualifying candidates, it is the point in time when the business owner, who has been coached to own the process, must now transition that strategy and set of beliefs—that energy—to the team.

As a business owner, it is your obligation, responsibility and privilege to guide the recruiting process in order to obtain talent that fits the culture and ultimately will drive your business toward its goals. Recruiting is a collaborative process that is supported by HR or a similar resource. It starts at the top with a strategic direction. Recruiting requires prerequisite activities, including building a hiring committee of stakeholders who define the criteria of a right-fit candidate. The hiring committee sets the strategic tone for the entire talent acquisition process, which houses the first three centers of excellence: recruiting, selection and onboarding.

Think first about your own recruiting process. Even if you feel like you're at par in the recruiting game, that's not winning. Anyone can hire poor or average performers. The mark of an effective recruiting process is that it is built to qualify top candidates, who are then developed into high-performing employees. If this is not the case for you, it's time to retool. It's time to figure out what's working, what's not, and identify exactly why substandard performers are seeping into the organization.

Again, recruiting focuses on filling the pipeline with qualified, talented candidates. That pool feeds the Selection process, which ultimately results in selecting top talent and onboarding them effectively—then training, developing and investing in them in the Strategic Talent Development corridor.

Many companies have a set of hiring activities, but effective recruiting involves engaging the company's leaders who are prepared to tease out the unique talents candidates possess. Your recruiting process is designed for your company. It is designed by the owner to foster the culture and drive the strategy. The owner sets the tone for how leaders go about bringing in talent with the skills, attributes and potential that will advance the company's objectives.

What businesses must understand now is, yesterday's recruiting doesn't work in today's highly networked, specialized and rapidly changing business world.

A Talent Management Approach to Recruiting

Recruiting in the Talent Acquisition corridor should be strategic not tactical, transformative not transactional. This is the first step in a series of getting to know someone. You are inviting them to get to know your company. The standard you set is also a message you send to candidates and to existing employees. Who you bring in for interviews sends a message to your existing team.

Consider how those conducting interviews on your company's behalf feel if the candidates vying for positions do not meet their own standards? They might wonder if they will have to do all of the work at the company—if their talents are being overlooked because the business is entertaining candidates who seem less than adequate. There are a myriad of implications resulting from a weak candidate pool created by ineffective recruiting. Owners need to take a good hard look at whom they allow into that candidate pool in the first place.

So, how long will this take, you're wondering. As for recruiting being an efficient process—there is a difference between hasty and efficient. Once upon a time, there was no distinction made for Selection, or even Onboarding, for that matter. It was all lumped together under Recruiting. Lumping everything together has had terrible consequences, not the least of which is forfeiting authentic interactions for a drive-thru window. We've just confused efficient with haste, which has caused the hiring process to be too hasty to adequately vet talent. It became a numbers game and recruiters believed the cream would naturally rise to the top. A recruiting process that is strategically designed to attract talent who meet criteria is efficient and effective.

Business owners have long realized that what they've been doing all along just doesn't produce good hiring decisions. And they've given up on figuring out how to do it right. They explain a mediocre hire with weak justifications: No one good wants to commute to my office out in the boonies. No one is specialized enough. No one is willing to jump ship and come to a new company like ours—and so on. So, many owners have given up on even believing they can acquire top talent because if quality people existed, wouldn't they have found them? Wouldn't they have figured this out by now? That's the type of thinking Strategic Talent Management turns around

But it doesn't stop there. Hiring with old equipment produces mediocre results, whereas a Recruiting strategy yields top talent.

Case Study: Setting the Table

The following insights are from a fine-foods supplier that began the Strategic Talent Management journey with recruiting—a "pain" that was holding back ambitious growth. The organization's initial goal was to attract and hire more qualified, inspired candidates who were in tune with their mission. You'd think that's what any solid recruiting process would yield, but that was just not the case.

The people in our organization were an unwitting barrier to our ability to achieve growth. Our company desperately needed to upgrade talent in several areas

across the organization—our expectations for key positions were significantly higher than the results we were getting.

Looking back over our first ten years, we were thinking short term and pinching our pennies. We were hiring one job at a time. We weren't thinking about building a team. I mean, I knew we wanted smart, ambitious, committed employees, and we fully intended to hire them. I didn't realize this then, but our interviewing practices actually aided and abetted bad hiring decisions.

Rather than ask candidates to answer questions, we seemed to tell them what we wanted to hear. In our effort to find out if the candidate could do the job, our questions inadvertently told the candidate what we were seeking in their answers. We had no way of gauging the quality or accuracy of the candidates' answers.

You can imagine that every single candidate "wowed" us! Before we knew it, we had a bunch of people with a bunch of titles, sitting at a bunch of desks underperforming. We had about three iterations of this until our product had reached a new level of customer for whom our team would NOT be able to perform.

Our process was filled with holes. We thought, "These people aren't working out." We knew the repetition of our failed recruiting had become detrimental to our growth. We had to stop starting from scratch every time with our recruiting if we were going to continue meeting our 40-percent annual growth benchmark.

We panicked, realizing we needed a radical overhaul and fast. But then we panicked again, realizing we didn't know who to go to for help. We had a hard time establishing a "hiring committee" because we were so anemic of talent. So, we tried something different. We used this methodology, changed our mindset, completely altered the way we engaged candidates, and hired three heavy hitters for key positions back to back. Now, we acknowledge that hiring and Strategic Talent Management is the most important thing we do as a fast-growing company.

Get Real with Recruiting: Stop Getting False Positives

Let's say recruiting at your company is fairly basic—you've done it the same way for some time. The hiring process seems efficient, beginning with rounding up candidates using a combination of online tools and a recruiter. Then the management team holds a series of interviews with a group of the most impressive candidates from your pool. From there, a few finalists are selected from the pick of the crop, and maybe a selection test is administered to help leaders choose who will ultimately win the position.

This recruiting process has brought in some of the company's top players; and, unfortunately, some of its low-performing employees who are dragging down morale and inhibiting the entire organization's growth potential.

The recruiting process is efficient but not effective. Why?

The candidates interviewing for open positions were qualified with a generic list of criteria, which couldn't possibly be teasing out the "A players." If you don't start by qualifying top talent for your pool, you can't expect to end with top talent when you get to selection. Where are the *A players* going to interview if not at your company? Remember that the reverse is also true: *A players* look for *A companies*. Does your hiring process reflect an A company? These are not rhetorical questions. You should expect to be able to answer them. And you should be dismayed (and motivated) if you don't have the answers you want.

The source of the talent employed at your company today is a reflection of the candidate pool you created during the Recruiting process. Filling that pool with A players requires a strategic approach to recruiting—and time. Strategic recruiting is an intense process that requires more resources and personal involvement than most owners may want to commit. That is, perhaps, why recruiting goes awry. The irony is, hiring the wrong person is a huge expense of your money, time, resources and growth potential. Strategic Talent Management is an investment in all those line items.

Business owners need to look at talent acquisition just as they would look at acquiring a business for expansion. High-level due diligence during recruiting yields the right hire. Picking the right candidate to grow your business is like picking the right company to expand it. Due diligence reduces risk and increases reward, and should be one of the most important aspects of a leader's job since it is the process of bringing new blood, ideas and skills into the business. And if that isn't enough, Recruiting is intricately linked to succession planning, to promoting talent and beating the competition.

- Acquiring talent is a basic, and critical building block of a business—the foundation. You need outstanding players to survive—to achieve. That's how serious recruiting is to the Talent Management process.
- You'll begin by agreeing on the recruiting criteria, screening the applicants, teasing out uncommon

talent, and then gleaning valuable intelligence during the Selection process with authentic touchpoints. The more time you spend with candidates, the better. These refinements are the difference between a method for due diligence and a rote, off-the-shelf hiring schedule.

- You'll challenge old assumptions that weaken your organization, such as: we'll lose the best candidate if we take too much time; we'll scare off quality people; we'll make the process too demanding; we'll frustrate our own employees if we keep the job open too long; and so on.

Recruiting Touches Everything that Follows

Recruiting is the foundation of the Strategic Talent Management process because without the infrastructure— the pipeline to filter out and usher in qualified prospects that will fill your pool of applicants—you're basically fishing in a swamp. Before recruiting is launched, a hiring committee must be formed. This committee essentially acts as the gatekeeper of the recruiting process. They, along with the owner, collectively set the hiring criteria for the recruiter, who fills the pipeline with candidates. Then, the Acquisition process unfolds into the Selection center of excellence with some or all of the following key elements:

Recruiting: Filling the pipeline with highly qualified candidates.
- Hiring Committee is assembled to set specific hiring criteria to be used in the steps that follow.
- Preliminary screening of candidates by the hiring manager or Human Resources.
- Qualifying online candidate survey.

Selection: Multiple, diverse and varied interactions with candidates, along with thoughtful and rigorous exchange of intellectual capital among the hiring committee.

- Structured interviews
- Unstructured interviews
- Group or panel interviews
- Selection assessments conducted by an external assessor
- A host of other steps to verify well-qualified candidates

Onboarding: Taking everything you learned about the candidate you selected (or promoted) and translating the data, insights and observations into a thorough Onboarding plan for his or her first 90 days.

Start with a Hiring Committee

A strong, diverse hiring committee that is dedicated to the process is necessary for recruiting qualified prospects, and properly vetting them during the Selection process to reveal top talent. Before a job is even posted, you assemble a hiring committee of individuals who participate in the process.

First, let's talk about the role of the hiring committee before and during Acquisition. The hiring committee's job is: 1) to define hiring criteria before the search is launched; 2) conduct various types of interviews during the selection process; 3) compile meaningful data for rigorous discussion with the committee; and 4) select a top candidate or continue the search with a new pipeline of qualified candidates. Each individual on the hiring committee should be dedicated to upholding the integrity of the recruiting and selection processes.

Who's involved in the hiring committee? It should include key stakeholders: human resources and managers from within and outside of the department hiring. Beyond that, it can be a good idea to include an employee who is outside of the department for which you are hiring, in a panel-discussion-style interview with a candidate. Consider including a colleague whose work may be impacted by the role of the new hire, but who is not necessarily responsible for overseeing their work. Think about who will often interact with this new hire. These are stakeholders, and by getting them onboard during the talent Acquisition process, you give your team an opportunity to share their expectations and hopes for a new hire. You will also minimize the risk of having competing objectives among stakeholders, who all want a piece of the new hire. Once the hiring committee is assembled, and comes to consensus on hiring criteria, the process is turned over to either an HR resource or someone from the hiring committee who will conduct the preliminary screening, and design a candidate survey to qualify candidates for the pool. Then during the Selection phase, collective involvement provides a more diverse perspective of a candidate's leadership capabilities than a one-on-one interview with a single executive.

Setting Hiring Standards

While the hiring committee meets to determine hiring criteria, its participants should consider the questions that each will ask during structured interviews, and how they will take notes during the structured interviews so that the intelligence captured can be shared in a useful and consistent manner. How will they come to consensus to agree on a final candidate? What questions will the hiring committee ask individuals, and how must candidates respond to be considered a "fit" for the job? Set the rules from the outset in terms of each individual's expectations for the hire. Establish a common ground.

Here are some points the hiring committee might consider as the qualifications for the position are defined, and while filling the candidate pool.

- What type of people matter to our business?
- Where are we falling short with talent?
- Are there people already working in the organization who can be developed or is the well dry? How do we determine this?
- What have been a few of our company's biggest hiring mistakes?
- What qualities do and do not work in our culture?
- What are the core competencies of this position?
- What skills are required to produce in the job?
- What attributes are required to fit the culture?
- How might this position change in three years, and what competencies will be needed for the future?
- What types of new opportunities in the company could this position lead to?

The answers to these questions shape a list of characteristics and values you'll seek in the individuals you hire. When properly executed and tailored, your Recruiting process—and the entire talent Acquisition corridor—will give you the confidence to trust your gut completely because your instincts will be backed by a system of due diligence and accurate reporting. This list of points will help the hiring committee come to consensus on the hiring criteria.

Consensus and the Hiring Committee

During Recruiting, you are using agreed upon criteria to fill the pool with qualified candidates. These criteria will determine candidates' general fit, including assessing biographical data, functional skills and professionalism. It will also gauge interest and motivation. Additionally, you might add a qualifying survey to further assess commitment. The purpose: to ensure the candidate meets basic standards and requirements before progressing to the next steps in the Selection process. Anyone who falls out now is self-selecting out, and that's a win.

Coming to consensus is hard work. As a team comes to consensus, they must first recognize they have differences of opinion. Unpracticed teams revert to defending personal views rather than expanding the group's thinking. However, if the committee deflects from the hard work of coming to consensus with their peers, the burden will be deflected to the candidate.

The risks of not having agreement are new hires have multiple masters who lead with competing agendas. This is what it means to set someone up for failure. Consensus is a convergence of implicit and explicit thinking—making sure what everyone expects from a candidate aligns with what everyone knows through interviews, reference checks, assessments and other tools. Benchmarking surveys may be used to facilitate consensus and gather information about what hiring committee members think. Then, those responses are compared and discussed to determine what is required to come to a consensus. Without true consensus— that means no settling—there is risk of hiring someone who eventually will fail at the business. This is as much a team-building activity for your leaders as it is teaching them to accept accountability for the people they hire.

The more the hiring committee interacts with the candidates, the better. The more varied the interactions with candidates, the better. The more touchpoints and authentic experiences your team has with candidates before a hire, the better. Remember, the goal is for each interviewer to gather information that is then shared, compared and discussed during debrief meetings.

Case Study: Lessons Learned

As for the fine-foods company we introduced earlier, the CEO and his leadership team learned a few valuable lessons pertaining to mistakes they were making with Recruiting and how they learned to do it right using Strategic Talent Management.

1) ***Agree on the Criteria.*** *The first time through the new process, we agreed on the criteria for qualifying candidates. We took the time to refine the job description and set clear goals for the position we were hiring for. We agreed on exactly the skills required to fulfill that role and the interpersonal attributes that would fit into our culture. Skills + attributes = a sure win.*

We scoured through résumés, closely screened qualified candidates, and critiqued our short list of top candidates. We were pretty much ready to pull the trigger on the better of two great candidates, when we decided to look back over our new process to make sure we had adhered to each step. That's when we realized we forgot to evaluate the capacity these candidates had to grow in the organization, to learn new things and take on a broader scope of responsibility someday. We assessed skills and aptitude. We assessed the attributes for fit. But we missed assessing for potential.

Honestly, as a team we were split. Half said, "Pull the trigger; hire one of the two." The other half said, "Follow our new standards; interview both candidates further." Finally, we agreed to extend the selection process. While our two candidates were ready to be selected, they seemed to appreciate our explicit desire not to make a mistake—after all we were protecting them as well.

When we fail to tailor the recruiting process and launch it as part of an overall Talent Management initiative, then we hire for the now vs. hiring for the future. We bring on people who can do the job today rather than ushering in talent with the capabilities to grow and forward our company's mission. We fill holes rather than fill roles.

2) **Screen the Applicants.** *Our approach to hiring and interviewing was just wrong. It was not going to achieve the real goal, which is to know and to understand the person, to know and to understand if they have the core competencies to do the job, and to know and understand whether they fit in the role and in the company, into our culture. None of that was happening. Candidates seemed good, sounded good, had the right background, and we made hiring decisions right away. We didn't know what we were looking for, and we wouldn't have known how to uncover it. Our process was weak.*

Leaders should take great care when selecting the interview questions they pose to candidates. Go beyond the basic, calculated questions that generate practiced generic responses. This results in prompted responses, canned answers. Simply put, off-the-shelf interviews are ineffective for gathering authentic insight during Talent Acquisition. They are great at bringing out the robot in your candidate. They do nothing to initiate spontaneous responses—to spark authentic dialogue. You've got to get real before hiring people into your business if you expect them to perform.

*3) **Tease Out Uncommon Talent.** We narrowed our candidates to two finalists, both of whom were highly qualified for the position. We started with 50 résumés, screened those to 20 candidates and whittled that group down to seven who had on-site interviews. And then we picked two, who took online assessments, returned for a panel discussion and more unstructured conversations. These two were the stars.*

As the team talked more, we shared more impressions, more thoroughly analyzed the online assessment results and the writing samples, we saw glaring red flags. In the end, we hired neither candidate, and went back to the recruiting process again smarter. We dodged the bullet. We could have made a huge mistake that would have cost our company a lot of money, time and resources. How do you backup and re-do a hire like that? You don't. It just fails and you feel stuck and, well, your entire organization feels the drain and drag.

We found an immensely qualified VP in the next round. Not only with aptitude, attitude and potential, but entrepreneurial at the core, and a foodie to boot!

Your company doesn't settle on sub-par materials or deliver mediocre services. You don't promise customers just an *OK* experience. So why should your hiring mentality be accepting of "what's out there" because you'll take what you can get? How does that recruiting attitude help your company realize growth potential? It doesn't.

Owners must take an approach where they connect with candidates and peel away the layers to find out what they're getting before you buy in. Isn't that the way you'd vet any vendor?

Enrich the Recruiting Process: The ROI

Why is recruiting the most important job you have as the leader of your company? Well for one, the cost of doing it poorly could put you out of business. The total cost of recruiting the wrong employee including hiring, total compensation, severance pay, time, resources, morale, reputation, customers, confidence and other factors like legal fees, can total up to $840,000 for a mid-level manager who works for 2.5 year and then is terminated and replaced (J. Sundberg, *The Undercover Recruiter*).

Dun and Bradstreet says it costs as much as 150 percent of salary to replace a management position. Hiring the wrong person is costly, and then you're starting from scratch. If the recruiting process is no different than last time, you can expect the same results. It's the old, "If you always do what you've always done, you'll always get what you've always got."

Now, consider the revenue you could have generated if you had hired the right person for the role.

Strategic Talent Management provides more value, more return-on-investment for an owner's recruiting dollars. Meanwhile, Recruiting is supported by a strong Training initiative, which we discuss in Strategic Talent Development beginning on page 87. When leaders can show candidates that they have a learning organization that creates opportunities for successful employees to grow and move beyond their positions into new roles—a ladder that employees can climb because of your company's training initiatives—an organization will attract premium candidates.

Talent Insight:

The hiring committee is, in essence, scouting for top players. If the hiring committee feels like they are involved in something as exciting as the NFL draft, or are judges on American Idol, then you're on to something. But if they feel it is perfunctory, or worse a waste of time, then you're leaving money on the table.

Selection: The Talent Deep Dive

Rigorous Selection teases out top talent and, ultimately, is a high form of risk management in the hiring process. Don't be afraid that a thorough Selection process will scare off your perfect candidate, because just the opposite is true. A rigorous Selection process will intrigue top performers and be a warning to mediocre performers. The Selection process accurately evaluates function, attitude and potential, and gets beyond a candidate's façade. It also reveals to each candidate your company's commitment to excellence and the high performance standards required of your people. Since top talent usually has choices, too, you want them to want you.

An intensive Selection process will give top performers a stage to compete and perform—and these top performers will value the investment you put into a process, because it is of critical importance to them, too. A candidate who is the right fit will opt in to this process and fully engage. After all, top talent is always eager to perform. The rigor intrigues them. The rigor shows you're truly interested. The rigor allows them the platform to showcase how they think about what they love. The rigor gives them a chance to imagine the competition and to outperform them. They won't feel lucky to get the job; they'll know they've been selected for it. It is a tremendous opportunity to create a collaborative environment for thoughtfully interviewing candidates, and for forming a hiring committee that will conduct thorough selection discussions.

The truth is, every time you invite a candidate to interview, you should expect to be interviewed, too. Top talent is just as concerned about choosing the wrong company and derailing their upward trajectory as you are about hiring someone who won't perform to your standards or match your culture. The road goes both ways.

A thorough, deep Selection process will stop the hiring treadmill.

Maybe you're familiar with this scenario? Your company whittles down a pool of candidates to three or five prospects, all highly qualified top performers with impressive résumés and references. These individuals pass initial screening with flying colors—they've got the skills, their salary expectations are in line with yours, and their experiences reflect the type of work you'd like to see them execute at your operation. Now, it's time for Selection (at this point, any of these candidates is a shoo-in, you figure).

You conduct a few standard interviews confirming the résumé and inquiring with your favorite interview questions. Then, you hire your new employee based on the results. The system is foolproof. So it seems.

But about six months after the employee joins your team, there are some real problems. The person is not a cultural fit, and you realize this when key managers hint, during separate occasions, that the person's performance is not meeting expectations. These are generally off-handed remarks. Or, perhaps nothing is said at all. Or HR is blamed. Then, an overall feeling of productivity malaise sets in.

What's the problem? You wonder how this person could be failing at your organization when the hiring process included screening and testing. Now begins the process of: 1) figuring out how to work with this person to change their ways; 2) moving them to another area of the organization hoping they can thrive in a different role, or; 3) figuring out how you can cut ties. Then, it's back to square one with recruiting.

Does this cycle sound familiar?

Many businesses are stuck on a hiring treadmill in part because their Selection process lacks the due diligence and deep-dive intensity it deserves. You wouldn't acquire a business or work with a vendor without doing a great deal of research, including personal conversations to ensure a proper fit. Due diligence and that deep reporting requires a significant time commitment. Sure, it is exhausting at times. The Selection process is a team approach, driven by the owner, facilitated by HR or the hiring manager, during which interviewers collect intellectual capital from candidates that is shared and compared, during committee meetings.

Talent Due Diligence

You know that talent acquisition is critical to your company's success and sustainability. Business growth is dependent on positioning people into roles where they will succeed. Right talent, right role. Going beyond that, you want the people you hire to exceed the expectations you set for them. For example, talent you hire to fulfill a vice president of operations position should seek to surpass the job description required of that role. This should show up in the Performance Management phase, so he or she can be mobilized for succession planning, with the intention of building your organization's bench strength.

Ultimately, Talent Acquisition is three-pronged (Recruiting, Selection, Onboarding), beginning with Recruiting, which is to fill a pool of qualified candidates and screen them with unexpected and authentic exercises or surveys. In Recruiting, we illustrated how a fresh approach to recruiting will attract a stronger, more qualified pool of talent. But once you have that pool, then what? How do you dig deeper and unearth authentic responses of an engaged set of individuals who could be your next high performer, how do you make an informed hiring decision?

The Selection process is your due diligence. Selection involves all of the touchpoints: initial screening; in-depth, structured interviews to gain insight into a person's business acumen; deep-dive interviews, during which conversations focus on leadership, problem solving, self-confidence and emotional intelligence, and selection tools that assess a candidate's personality and preferences, while gauging aptitude and potential. It is a series of touchpoints that progresses from preliminary to scripted to engaged. Each one of these touchpoints helps you to know and to understand the candidate, and helps the candidate to know and understand you, the role and the company.

Implementing a system for Selection is critical to the Talent Acquisition process. Here, a CEO lays out some of the company's inherent hiring challenges by sharing the personnel treadmill that was resulting because of recruiting, selecting and onboarding people who were not a cultural fit:

Hiring people for a growing company is arguably the most critical thing we do. Where we were missing the ball was finding candidates that fit into our culture. We weren't aligning our hiring with our culture, and we intuitively knew it and felt it. We did not have a model for screening candidates—we did not have a structure, a repeatable process for filtering candidates.

Employees' skills were there, their aptitude was strong, but the leadership style and work ethic were not. The internal pool of talent was empty come promotion time. Ideally you want to nurture a valuable workforce so 60 to 70 percent of recruiting efforts happen from within the organization. You want to hire from your own talent pool rather than hitting the streets time and again. You want to depend on the people you already have to grow with the company. This is not possible if the people you bring on in the first place are just filling openings.

Why are business owners more willing to pay external recruiters a third of base to fill a position, but so unwilling to invest in developing existing talent? I am not saying these two opportunities are mutually exclusive. But I believe that business owners aren't aware of this contradiction.

This particular company was prepared to make a decision between two candidates who had been vetted through interviews. It turns out, neither candidate was hired. And, we turned the company's hiring process upside down in a way that now allows the organization to select people who will excel in its culture.

I realized that what we had been doing throughout my entire career was inherently the problem—our approach to hiring and interviewing was just wrong.

By definition, it was not going to achieve the real goal, which is to know and understand the person, and to understand whether they fit into the role in the company, into our culture. None of that was really happening. If a candidate felt good, seemed right and had the appropriate background, we hired the person right away. It was a crap-shoot approach.

I understood our problem. I had people in my organization who were holding back our growth. You hit certain cycles in the life of your company where it becomes abundantly clear that some of the people in the organization are not a fit, and at the same time that the organization is not where you want it to be. I recognized that clearly.

Selection is critical to a company's ability to grow and prosper. It's an intense, important process of gathering intelligence before you make the serious investment in a person. Selection is tied to the financial success of a company because we need people who elevate our organization, who help grow it. People power our businesses, from a financial and organizational perspective. There is a direct people and profit connection.

Authentic Touchpoints

Selection with a Strategic Talent Management mindset challenges you to rethink the way you interview candidates. It forces you to dig deeper and find out what makes each final candidate tick. Business owners need to find out about how candidates respond in any situation so they can be sure individuals being considered for employment will thrive in the culture and, ideally, exceed job expectations. As owners, you want your employees to take your business to a higher level. Why should we expect anything less?

Many companies act on impulse after a fairly lightweight interview process—maybe a phone conversation followed by an in-person interview. So, the owner signals the green light: the candidate feels right and the hire is made. There is no rigorous screening process during recruiting or online surveys that produce writing samples that really peel away the top layers. The approach is: meets general qualifications, can hold a conversation, has a résumé that seems to prove experience, passes the background check, done. Recruiting focuses on whittling a candidate pool down to a short list, figuring in the job description, budget and any deal-breakers—will the person relocate to your city? Does the candidate hold a certain degree or have specific certifications or experience? Will the candidate show up on time?

Then the interview happens and bare minimum questions are lobbed to the candidate. Again, it's like theater: the actors play their parts. You ask about the candidate's' weaknesses; the candidate answers by turning their sore points into positives. You want to know why the person desires to work at your company, and the individual provides something about what they read on your website—polished yet perfunctory—and you check off that question as done.

If your interview process is so predictable that candidates can be coached in advance on how to answer the questions, the talent pool is way too shallow.

The more interactions an owner has with candidates, the richer the Acquisition process. Every touchpoint peels away a layer. The more leaders engage candidates in "off-road" scenarios—that is, engagements that happen beyond the conference room—the more likely they are to uncover the real essence of individuals vying for that open position.

In the Selection process, rethink the place and time, and the questions posed during interviews.

Structured interviews extract historical data, real-life experiences and specific types of situations and circumstances, as well as the candidate's ability to self-evaluate, learn from mistakes and assert successes. Behavioral-based questions are introduced in order to go beyond the bullets on a résumé, to narrate the résumé, verify accuracy of the résumé, assess for depth of experience. These questions are formatted in a way that require the candidate to recount experiences chronologically, provide answers systematically and offer a self-evaluation. At the same time, this structured approach helps interviewers to take good notes that can be compared, apples to apples, with others on the hiring committee. And these questions can be assigned in advance to each interview so there are no overlaps and redundancies with the questions the interviewers ask.

Outcome goal: Select the top talent/best fit

Mindset: Create an experience that is respectful and positive for every candidate regardless of hiring decision.

It's a Two-Way Street

➤ Engage candidates so they can perform well. You will have multiple touchpoints so candidates have a chance to perform well over time, which indicates consistency and reliability.

➤ Make sure your company puts its best foot forward. Your ability to demonstrate consistency between your behaviors and your company's culture starts now.

Part HR : Part Marketing

➤ Prepare the hiring committee so no two interviews are asking overlapping questions.

➤ Create a respectful and positive experience that compels candidates to share their experience with your company to those outside your company.

➤ Let candidates know what to expect as follow up to each step of the selection process. Leaving candidates hanging is a sign that you are underperforming.

Set the Tone

➤ Introduce yourself, describe your role, how you interact with the position being filled. Share something about yourself that is relatable. Be approachable.

➤ Confirm the time allotted and how many questions you might ask, and suggest they describe what they've done as well as how they think through situations.

➤ Leave time for the candidate to ask questions. Be transparent and open.

It's A Team Sport

➤ Each interviewer should obtain high-quality information to share with the hiring committee.

➤ Sharing quality information transforms data into intellectual capital, which is critical for making accurate hiring decisions.

Figure 8: Selection Touchpoints

These are the instructions the interview provides to prepare the candidate for the questions.

Describe the Situation or Task:

- Based on the question asked, describe a situation that you were in or that required your attention. Please reference a specific event or situation, not a general description of what you would do or would have done.

Describe the Action You Took:

- Continuing from the situation, describe the action you took, the impact you had, the judgments you made, the thinking you applied.

Describe the Results You Achieved:

- Continuing from the actions you took, describe the outcome. What happened? How did the event conclude? What did you accomplish? What did you learn?

Sample Competency-Based Interview Questions (CBIQs): You can certainly develop your own questions. Keep in mind, you need to set up the question so it can be answered with the formula: Situation, Action, Outcome

1. *Accomplishments:* The standard you set is also a message you send, too.

2. *Decision Making:* Describe a time you had to make an unpopular decision. How was it received? How did you handle it?

3. *Delegating:* We cannot do everything ourselves. Give me an example of a time when you needed to delegate a task. Who did you delegate to, and was that determined?

4. ***Goal Setting:*** What important goals did you have in your last job? Exactly what were they, and what were your results?

5. ***Initiative:*** Tell me about times when you seized the opportunities, grabbed something and ran with it yourself.

6. ***Managing Others:*** Describe a time you managed an unreliable and inconsistent employee (or highly emotional or volatile employee)?

7. ***Motivating Others:*** Give an example of a time when your communication skills were powerful enough to influence the way others thought or acted, even in a very difficult situation.

8. ***Overcoming Adversity:*** Describe a time when you were not very satisfied or pleased with your performance. What did you do about it?

9. ***Self Awareness:*** Describe a time when you have been disappointed by your own behavior.

Focus on truly getting to know the candidates and what makes them tick. Play a board game. Discuss a thought leadership video (such as a TED talk). Email the candidate an article and invite an e-mail discussion, casually. Share some news and ask: What do you think about this? Invite them to dinner. Invite their spouse, too. Consider sharing one of your own interests with the candidate—art, music, sports, fine dining, whatever that may be. Remember, this candidate could become part of an inner circle of trust at your company. As the business owner, you deserve and need to know what makes this person tick. Selection should reveal candidates' true colors.

When companies conduct poor interviews, then every candidate interviews poorly. That's a lot of false negatives, meaning you might be passing on the very person you should ultimately hire. You have to create a black diamond recruiting course so you can see the great performers perform. We'll talk more about this in the Selection chapter.

Ensuring True Positives

1. *Set up:* two-way street; branding; being prepared, showing you care, getting to know each other.

2. *Structured interviews:* historical, attitude and skill and business acumen; behavior-based interview questions (BBIQs); taking notes to ensure comparison can be made and intellectual capital can be used.

3. *Unstructured Interviews:* engaged, authentic, how do you think, engage in the moment and unrehearsed, share, collaborate, anticipate and conjecture (journals, real-time dilemmas, etc.).

4. *Reconvene the hiring committee for decision making*: compare notes, rigorous discussion, leave no stone unturned, challenge each other, push the envelope, take nothing at face value.

5. *Repurpose* all the information gleaned from the Selection process into an onboarding plan that will accelerate the new hire's ability to assimilate into the culture and earn credibility with the team to become efficient and productive for the long term.

Selection happens after a pool of candidates is assembled and vetted. Selection is the deep dive. This is not a transactional process. Now that you have an assembly of qualified individuals, you can uncover the layers of each finalist to learn what makes the prospect tick. Selection in the Strategic Talent Management continuum emphasizes meaningful experiences.

What is appropriate and effective for your business depends entirely on your culture and comfort level. Here, we provide a framework, not an off-the-shelf process. That means there is work involved on the part of the owner/CEO, and some soul searching.

Set the Tone for Selection

The Selection process illustrates a day-in-the-life at the company and confirms that candidates get a clear picture of expectations. The organization and its leaders, in turn, gain a deeper perspective of the talent and potential during interviews and can make informed, high-quality, sound hiring decisions. The manner in which Selection is conducted, from the place to people involved, is highly personal and must suit a company's culture and goals. Selection ultimately sets the stage for Talent Acquisition success.

At the same time, the Selection process touches other aspects of an organization, well beyond the act of sourcing human capital. Consider marketing, for example. During Selection, a company opens its doors so people can see the inner-workings of the company, what the company stands for, what it values. The candidates who are entertained for the position open a vein. There's no type of marketing or advertising that bares your organization's soul quite like a solid Selection process.

Candidates leave the process with an impression, whether they are hired or not. They're talking about their experience interviewing with your company to other people, too. The Selection environment plays a significant role in ensuring that an organization's brand is preserved, and perhaps elevated, during this process. Selection must be executed with integrity, respect, honesty, courage and curiosity.

There is a manner in which Selection should be conducted to assure the process's success, and to even propel your organization's brand in the process. In contrast, when companies neglect candidates for weeks at a time during the process and treat them dismissively, they are essentially tossing marketing dollars down the drain. When interviewers show up unprepared, having scanned the résumé moments before walking into the interview, and make a bad impression on candidates, you're left with damage control—spending dollars to resurrect a poor image.

A Sense of Place: Most meetings with candidates will be held at your place of business, in a conference room or office environment. This gives the candidate an opportunity to see the facility, tour it and feel it. However, do not be limited by convention. Remember, the goal is to gain a deeper understanding of each candidate and have meaningful interactions prior to a hiring decision. You're aiming for authentic experiences that will reveal a person's character and values. This process requires stepping outside of the usual mental boundaries we place on Selection, and also beyond the physical boundaries of place. You set the rules for the Selection environment.

Heavy Lifting

Interviews: Structured interviews with candidates involve key stakeholders and are generally conducted in a traditional environment. Now that the candidate has passed the screening interview, your goal is to introduce this person to stakeholders within the organization and to begin peeling back the layers with various types of interactions that prompt the candidate to discuss personal work experiences and achievements—along with challenges and how those were mastered.

Tailor Interview Questions: The crux of an effective, tailored Selection process are meaningful interviews with candidates that reveal how they solve problems, lead a team, respond in adverse situations—how they will fit into your culture. There are various levels of questions you will ask: Preliminary (remedial) questions that are asked during Recruiting to screen candidates; structured interviews that draw out candidates' experiences; and engaged interviews that include open-ended questions that are intended to draw out impromptu, what-if thinking—analytical, anticipatory thinking.

Structured questions are designed to draw out candidates' experiences. These questions give candidates little opportunity for embellishment—they provide opportunities for candidates to describe real-life situations from beginning to end, in detail. This gives an interviewer the benefit of learning how candidates view challenges, how they solve problems, and their perception of the outcomes of the situations described. These questions also help candidates recollect specific people, places and time. You can't fake that stuff! This approach helps the hiring committee gather candidates' responses in a consistent format so information can be shared during debrief meetings.

Engaged interview questions will gauge candidates' willingness to assert opinions or unique perspectives on issues. These interviews are effectively conducted in a panel format, which will heighten the intensity and require candidates to think on their feet. You may use a case study or other material that provides a basis for speculating, anticipating, forming opinions and perspectives. This is not designed to be a test of wits, but more a framework for how this candidate engages ideas in the moment.

As candidates progress from formal to more genuine interactions during the interview process, the hiring manager reveals more about the job: how the person will be expected to lead, the strengths they must bring, and the type of talent required to round out the team and fit the culture. These interviews evolve into a conversation between candidates and interviewers/the hiring manager.

During the entire interview process, CBIQs are used to elicit responses that demonstrate a candidate has (or has not) accomplished given tasks. The interview questions should be divided among interviewers so the hiring committee gains a broad base of knowledge about each candidate. The team may agree on a set of questions that each will ask in order to compare responses given to each interviewer.

The interview questions should be divided among interviewers to the hiring committee gains a broad base of knowledge about each candidate. The team may agree on a set of questions that each will ask in order to compare responses given to each interviewer (different questions about leadership, for example).

As we have emphasized along this journey, you the owner must steer this process. Your hiring committee must collaborate to design questions that align with the skills and values you believe the candidate should have in order to be considered for employment. You already asked preliminary questions during the recruiting phase to gauge the basic interest of the candidate. Now, follow with staged scripted questions that reveal candidates' competencies and allow you to compare them apples to apples. Engaged questions go a step further and help you observe the candidate's unique disposition, and determine whether they are a cultural fit. Finally, an exchange should occur that allows you, and the hiring committee, to mutually share conversation and discussion (and to ask each other questions). Here is where a candidate's potential is unlocked.

Once the questions are gathered, the real opportunity emerges when the team comes together to share and compare intellectual capital each interviewer collected. When the hiring team meets and thoroughly discusses a candidate with the narrative captured by each interview, the interviewer must take it deeper and evolve the candidate's initial answer into a more intellectually revealing response.

As we noted, through the Selection process, the hiring committee is extracting information and preparing notes. The time candidates spend during the interview process will mold their entire experience working at your organization. And that, too, is why Selection is a great deal more than narrowing down top talent. It is a culture-affirming, revealing process where both parties strip down to what's important, what matters, and a decision is made about whether a future stakeholder is a fit.

Selection Assessments: The intelligence gleaned from multiple interviews is verified by the results of an assessment tool or a battery of assessments, which can include a personality inventory, an aptitude test, a job-specific assessment and a leadership test. These can be tie-breaker tools.

Assessments are most often facilitated by an external expert, who can administer, interpret and advise on selection decisions. These tools are meant to uncover and identify strengths, weaknesses, blind spots, preferences, motivators, leadership competencies and judgment. This is the type of information that is difficult to learn from interviews. The metrics derived from the assessments overlay the data extracted from the biographical materials and interviews, creating new data points. The comparisons made and the discussions that ensue further ensure a true positive and true negatives when making selection decisions.

Selection & the Talent Management Corridor

Ultimately, Selection within Strategic Talent Management is focused on building bench strength one individual at a time. A company can fully launch an effective recruiting process by engaging some of the company's stakeholders in the interview process. Panel interviews can be effective and peel back the layers of a candidate's experiences. And, unconventional touchpoints get you closer to a candidate's instinct, gut and purpose, therefore driving more-informed hiring decisions.

Talent Insight:

The best interview questions surface when the hiring committee members sit and share what they don't know, and wanted to know.
I always ask: "Why are you wondering about these topics? Ask about them directly."

Doubts and reservations about a candidate can be translated into curious questions that you ask the candidate directly.

Onboarding:
Generating Energy, From Day One

The first few days of an employee's life at a business represent a rare, untapped window of time where the new hire enters a fresh environment shining, inspired and ready to make a difference. The organization gets a shot in the arm; an instant infusion of talent and energy. Properly channeled and leveraged, this new-hire vitality and vigor can permeate the culture and positively impact people at all levels of your organization. This period of welcome and orientation is an incredible opportunity to revive your team. It's a one-time chance to roll out the red carpet for that new employee—to show your team that this promising, thoughtfully selected person matters. It should remind others of their first day, and if it was memorable (as it should be), then everyone will have something to share that revives them.

The process of orienting a new hire is formally called Onboarding. When done effectively, Onboarding will set the tone for the new employee's role, efficiently orient the person to the job and culture, cement the existing team, and improve the overall productivity of your operations.

Many organizations implement a watered-down Onboarding that has the potential of leaving their new blood feeling jilted at the altar. This is it? This is what I've been waiting for? I went through all that to get this? Clearly, this is not the impression any leader wants a new hire to gather on the first days, or any day for that matter.

Effective Onboarding accelerates productivity and generates energy. An employee hits the ground running the first day because he or she connected with the company's mindset at the first interview. Their first day was actually that initial interview, as they got to know your company better and began to learn about its culture. The training/onboarding process began during Recruiting. In fact, Onboarding is a continuation—albeit a more formal start—of the orientation that began when you opened the door to first speak with the candidate. Doesn't this mindset change the Talent Acquisition focus completely? Doesn't it underscore the value of a rigorous Recruiting and Selection process leading up to Onboarding? And, doesn't it make sense that doing so changes the Onboarding experience completely, because candidates are in the game before they ever start the job?

Research and conventional wisdom suggest that employees get about 90 days to prove themselves in a new job. The faster new hires feel welcome and prepared for their jobs, the faster they will be able to successfully contribute to the firm's mission. Let's talk about the cost of ineffective onboarding, in a word: turnover. According to a 2012 Allied Workforce Mobility Study, companies lose 25 percent of all new hires within a year. The average cost to fill one position is $11,000, the study says. Thirty percent of companies say it takes a year or longer for a new employee to reach full productivity, and 25 percent of respondents said they have no formal training program. Meanwhile, 60 percent do not set goals or milestones for new hires.

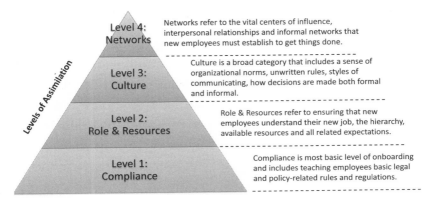

Figure 9: Onboarding—four levels of assimilation

Onboarding should be optimized to engage the new hire, express the value of this talent to the entire team, and integrate the person into the culture. This generates lasting, productive energy. This is onboarding the Strategic Talent Management way.

Optimize Onboarding

How Selection is executed directly impacts onboarding success. During the Selection process, you brought together a hiring committee or informal team that performed the assessments and conducted the interviews to help choose this employee. These stakeholders came to an agreement on what qualities and skills the new hire needs to perform in the position; and the expectations superiors, peers and the organization at-large have for this person as they work in their new role. Ultimately, the incoming employee is a new resource—and before he or she walks in the door, there should be a clearly communicated set of goals and objectives for that person.

Unfortunately, Onboarding is often merely, "Welcome to our company. Here's the coffee room. There are the restrooms. And this is your cube." It's basic orientation. Onboarding optimization requires resetting these behaviors and expectations, and setting goals. When Selection is conducted with a Strategic Talent Management mindset, as a critical working part of an overall plan to build bench strength, Onboarding becomes a powerful time when three things happen: 1) trust is built; 2) energy is created; and 3) productivity begins immediately. Ultimately, Onboarding is when the agreement between the company and candidate is met. The company can expect 100 percent from the new hire; and that individual can expect to fulfill career aspirations based on the opportunity.

Further, every bit of data gathered about the new hire during Recruiting and Selection is translated into the Onboarding plan. You invested in rigorous due diligence. The brilliance of that process is material that can and should be recycled for Onboarding—a continued return on your Strategic Talent Management investment. Here is how one company recognized that two false starts—new-hires that left 18 months after joining the organization—were the cause of a failed Talent Acquisition process.

Before Tom could transition the family business to his son, Mark, the fourth generation, a crucial step was necessary: backfilling Mark's position as head of operations. The plan was for Tom to move into the role of chairman, and for Mark to ascend to the position of CEO. But many steps were necessary before this succession plan could be executed, and finding the right fit for a key leadership role always looks easier on paper than it really is. Adding to the complexity was Tom and

Mark's distinctly different management styles, and they knew this. Tom was a benevolent leader who walked the shop floor and knew everyone's name and details about employees' lives and families. He had a for-the-people reputation. In return, his people were dedicated and hardworking, positive and grateful. It was important to have Tom's approval and to be seen as a team player.

Mark was a driven leader who asked lots of questions. He knew people by the quality of their work and their interest in advancing in the company. Mark made his employees feel useful and he had a reputation for being focused on results. In return Mark's people were conscientious and deliberate, hardworking and alert.

Together, Tom and Mark were a good team, and their different skills were complementary for the five years they prepared for the transition. They agreed early on that when Mark became CEO, his replacement would have a leadership profile more like Tom's and foster a similarly balanced partnership.

The question was, could someone within the organization fill the operations role? Two years into the five-year transition plan, Tom and Mark determined that none of the division vice presidents were a fit for the VP operations job that Mark would be leaving. So they decided to conduct a search through an executive recruiting firm—and the effort turned out to be a complete debacle. They had two false starts, actually bringing on candidates that left the company within 18 months of being hired. Tom and Mark were frustrated, confused and, quite frankly, embarrassed. They reached out to Tom's peer advisory group, and a member suggested coaching and Strategic Talent Management as a potential solution for shedding light on the recruiting problem and taking a different approach.

The process began with analyzing the situation: Did they hire the wrong recruiting firm? Were they seeking a leader to fill the operations position who did not exist? Did the new-hires leave so quickly because division heads were setting them up to fail? Mark speculated that his division vice presidents were looking for a candidate who would maintain the status quo. But Tom and Mark were seeking someone approachable like Tom, but tougher—someone who would push for accountability, like Mark did. The hiring missteps created some complicated, unintended consequences. One, the management team was becoming too powerful in the hiring decision; and two, Tom and Mark were beginning to feel that the company was not worthy of retaining a quality VP operations hire.

This discovery process sparked the reinvention of the company's talent acquisition process. They needed a better way of identifying, selecting and onboarding a new VP of operations. First, a hiring committee of key stakeholders was established. Through a series of facilitated conversations and a job survey, the team of leadership, management and human resources members came to consensus on the core capabilities for the VP operations. In retrospect, the team realized that they each had vastly different views and expectations for the position that were even contradictory. Competing agendas could have set up the prior two executives for failure.

The team also learned through this process that past interviews involved asking the same questions to the candidates. In two cases, the interviews had only reviewed the résumé five minutes before the interview. This lack of preparation was evidence that the managers were not engaged, and interviewers were unintentionally communicating to candidates that the company didn't care. As a result, hiring decisions were at risk for being random and out of control. This discourages top candidates from performing at their best during an interview.

Ultimately, the hiring committee came to consensus on the job profile of the VP operations, the interviewing process, the division of labor for the hiring committee, and the performance expectations that each member of the hiring committee diligently collect relevant data to compare with each other after their interviews.

The team agreed that the company could outsource the heavy lifting of recruiting to fill the candidate pool: identifying, screening and evaluating passive and active candidates. The recruiting firm was provided with clear directions concerning the position's core competencies, necessary leadership attributes and potential for growth and success the role could bring. The company was seeking someone who would fit the job requirements, culture and future potential for succession planning.

A benchmark was also identified for the recruiting process. "No casualties." Every candidate who touched the company would have a positive experience. Every candidate would walk out of an interview with a good feeling about the company. Ultimately, the talent acquisition process became more of a marketing initiative than a human resource initiative. The team took ownership and accountability for the success of *filling the VP operations role. And, they were proud of the new system for selecting a candidate. With this process, an ideal fit for the VP operations was identified and ushered through the interview and selection processes. And, with attention to the Onboarding process in the Strategic Talent Management process, the company successfully integrated the new hire into the company culture.*

Build Trust

Trust is a series of experiences among people that sets the tone for what can be expected. Trust is built during the Selection process, and it is cemented during Onboarding. The more interactions and opportunities you have to demonstrate your credibility, the deeper this trust will become, even during this early stage of a new employee's time at the company—literally, the first few days.

Trust is directly related to credibility, which is necessary if you are to influence your people in a positive way to drive the team towards meeting goals. If your new hire is a resource—and indeed, this is the case—that resource must be tapped by proving credibility and earning trust. This occurs during the Selection process with interviews that peel away the layers of a person and promote engagement and authentic sharing. The sharing goes both ways, as you and interviewees set expectations of the job, paint a true picture of the culture, address the company's strengths and weaknesses and how this role will bolster the organization.

During Onboarding, trust-building continues at a fast rate as soon as that new hire walks in the door. When the team is prepared to embrace the new talent as a resource who will help the organization grow and thrive (along with the people involved in it), then trust flourishes quickly. Trust empowers people to peak perform.

Create Energy

How have you prepared your people to welcome the incoming member of the team? What does your staff expect from this new person? Do they understand why the employee was hired? Why his or her talents are a match for the organization? I believe this is important information to share with your team before a new employee's first day on the job. At the very least, direct reports, colleagues who will work frequently alongside this new hire, and superiors should understand the value of the employee before he or she walks in the door.

Seeing the new hire as a resource before they start generates excitement among the team: We have a new member joining us who will help us do our jobs faster/ better/smarter and who will work with us to reach company goals/objectives/growth targets, etc. This positive measure of simply introducing and validating the hire to stakeholders goes a long way toward creating Onboarding energy. And as illustrated, when that person walks into the door on the first day, you want him or her to feel like this was the best decision both parties could have made. You want all new hires to feel (I'll say it again) that their presence matters.

Jumpstart Productivity

Effective Onboarding gets employees up to speed in minimal time—that means sparking productivity quickly, while there is energy and momentum and buy-in from team members. We all strive to find ways to maximize our time, because it is effectively the one resource we have no control over. We can't expand it. We can't grow more of it. We can't buy more of it (but we can sell it). Time is everything. Profitability is dependent on making the best use of time, and the people we employ in our businesses are responsible for using time wisely, producing capably and efficiently during the time they do have.

Now, are you checking your watch? Tapping your finger on your desk at the thought of this? Feeling a sense of urgency to motivate your team? When we onboard a new employee, every minute of their orientation counts.

We generate a 180-day plan, beginning from the Selection date, for this orientation period. And, if we have prepared them for their role during Selection, we are already ahead of the game because they'll onboard more efficiently. If we have built energy among the team, we are fast-forwarding the onboarding process by establishing early connections between the new hire and his or her new teammates. We've primed the pump.

Onboarding Checklist

The first eighteen months, the long-term onboarding period, are critical to a new employee's success and entire life at your organization. After that time, the employee will have been "baked," so to speak—he or she will have formed a role, an attitude, a way of doing things, whether or not it was what you intended. That is why Onboarding is absolutely critical to the Strategic Talent Management process. You can't have productive Onboarding without effective Selection. You can't move on and develop employees that were never properly onboarded—and if you do develop them, you'll find that you've got a lot of extra work to do.

So, what exactly needs to happen during Onboarding? This sample schedule is a reference. As with every Center of Excellence in the Strategic Talent Management process, you'll put your stamp on it. Use it as a resource, a loose outline. Customize it and collaborate with key stakeholders to determine how the Onboarding timeline aligns with your goals for productivity and growth.

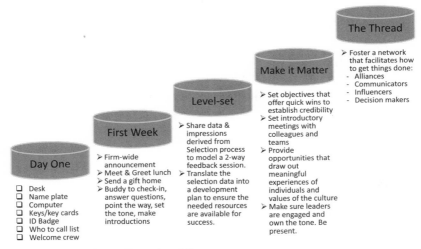

Figure 10: Onboarding checklist

Strategic Schedule of Introductions:

1:1s with direct reports

- Tell me what you're working on that you really enjoy and would not want to lose touch with.
- Tell me what you're doing that isn't enjoyable or isn't advancing in the way you want. Can I help?
- Is there an idea or project you've wanted to initiate but can't get any traction on? Can I help?

- In what ways could you feel more satisfied in your job?

1:1 with shared services
- What is your highest level of value to the business?
- How does your department succeed?
- How do you like to work with the departments you support?

1:1 with superiors
- What is your leadership style?
- How do you prefer to communicate?
- What things do I do that directly impact your objectives?

Regular check-ins:

1:1 with HR or sponsor
- Help advocate and navigate, and protect against bottle-necks

1:1 with hiring manager
- Facilitate relationships, ensure early wins, build confidence, reinforce commitment

---

Talent Insight:

The first day on the job is not the new employee's start date—it was the day that the initial interview was conducted and the individual was introduced to your company, your culture and your team. Onboarding happens throughout the Talent Acquisition process, beginning with rigorous Recruiting and careful Selection. During all this time, the candidate is becoming oriented to your values and mission so that when the official Onboarding time comes, he or she hits the ground running.

Corridor:
Development

In the Strategic Talent Management continuum, the Development Centers of Excellence (Training, Performance Management, Leadership Development) focus on creating an environment for people to do their best work, preparing them for success, and honing their talents to help grow the organization. Specifically, Training is enterprise-wide, Performance Management focuses on individuals, and Leadership Development is when the organization focuses on its top performers.

Training: The New School

Here are important questions to ask yourself: How is training being delivered at your organization? How are your people learning? What tools are you providing to facilitate engaged mindshare? So often, businesses owners are locked into the belief that you don't need to develop someone you hired to do a job. In other words, if someone needs to be developed, they're not right for the job. On the other hand, owners know that people need to develop on the job to grow, but they don't know how to tell the difference between someone with high potential or someone who is just tapped out.

Most training professionals acknowledge collaborative activities are critical for workplace learning, and when typical corporate training is deployed, workers tend to get frustrated and "check out." The old way of training doesn't produce the type of worker needed to succeed in today's networked society. That is, someone who is collaborative, who creates value, fulfills personal and company goals, is flexible and forward thinking.

There is a movement that is changing the way we work, the meaning we give to work and what we should expect from our careers. There's a radical paradigm shift that is altering the formal, rote training we applied during the Industrial Age into a network-based mindset that emphasizes knowledge and connection, and that really works for today's Information Age.

Similarly, training in Strategic Talent Management is not training how we know it. It is learning. You have a classroom of individuals, a group of distinctly different people with various skills and experiences. Each was hired for a different reason and purpose. Your people work differently, and they will perform differently—they think and learn differently. They connect differently. But, for the most part, we expect them to accept information that is routinely fed to them during basic orientations or procedural-based training sessions in the same way. We expect that they will soak in the training, then go out and do their jobs, and do them well.

With this method of training in practice, it's no surprise that the process is viewed as a chore for employees—a mandatory next-step after they are hired, and/or a requirement for updating skills. Too many employees go into training with an automatic-pilot attitude. And why should they approach it any other way if the classroom is a book-based, hierarchal environment where the trainer is dishing out information to trainees, who are listening and (supposedly) learning? What's more, this training typically lacks follow up, so what's the motivation for knowledge retention or engagement?

In a Strategic Talent Management framework, Training is an enterprise-wide campaign that sets the tone for your expectations of employees' performance. It is the foundation upon which you will eventually build Performance Management and Leadership Development. Training is also a Recruiting tool that attracts valuable players who desire a learning environment where employers invest in their success, and support their growth.

When we change the way training is formatted and delivered, we empower the people in our companies to engage, collaborate, think strategically and deploy their talents for the purpose of reaching the organization's goals.

Training is so much more than learning the ropes. Capturing the power of training involves creating an environment where interactive, progressive learning happens. We want to promote rigorous thought and challenge our people to challenge themselves. Then, training becomes a think-tank, a forum for innovation and discovery, for tapping potential.

Of course, aspects of training will require delivering important pieces of information that must be communicated: safety and compliance, benefits, company policies. But training must go beyond the pre-fabricated and off-the-shelf lesson modules and formality. Training in Strategic Talent Management will ensure that employees have the foundation for greater thinking and doing.

Re-Evaluate the Way We Train

We want to prepare our people to think critically and solve problems. Our people should question processes— the opposite of what antiquated training suggests—and then help design solutions to make our organizations better, faster, stronger and more profitable. That's why training has the power and the potential to serve as a platform for continuous learning. Training should be a learning mindset and environment that we create for our people. During training, we should be planting seeds. Then, the experiences we give our people will fortify that training and nurture personal growth and leadership development. We set a platform that evolves with the active participation from the learners.

There is a good, financial reason why organizations should maximize training—it's a significant investment. Corporations spend an average $1,067 per employee (2.7% of payroll) to deliver an average of 32 hours of formal training annually, according to The American Society for Training and Development. The majority of this reported training, 70%, is instructor-led, with the remainder delivered via technology.

The group also found that firms that invest $1,500 per employee in training, compared to those that spend $125, experience an average 24% higher gross profit margin and 218% higher revenue per employee.

Companies that spend more on training get more productivity from their people. The Cheesecake Factory spends about $2,000 per employee for training each year and reaps sales of $1,000 per square foot, which is more than twice the industry average. Further, the company has an employee retention rate about 15% better than the national average. Retention alone is not an indicator of employee engagement. Sometimes high retention is a sign that leadership is willing to carry dead weight. You must look deeper to understand the retention numbers.

Again, ask yourself how you are training your people? And, keep in mind, our networked society values social, informal learning, interactivity and collaboration. Sitting in a classroom in front of an instructor does very little to forward our success. This is not the Industrial Age. We are living in the

Network Era, where workers create the value, not machines. Training processes must be adapted to suit the competitive business environment. Do we want to teach our people to operate like a Commodore 64?

When we deliver generalized training, we get rote results and bored workers. Gallup reports that 49% of employees are not actively engaged, and 18% are actively disengaged. That means, about one out of five people you employ is actually working at not working. And half of your staff is just hanging out. Take a look at your payroll and decide if you can afford to fund dead weight.

Here's another reality with training the old way: the new generation just isn't going to buy in. As Baby Boomers exit the work force, they've got to pass down that knowledge somehow, some way. But the next generation of workers does not want to be spoon fed or talked at. Collaborative training, which engages people at all levels of the organization, is a solution for effective learning and ongoing professional and personal development. It's alive, relevant and interactive. In this way, training becomes an opportunity at your company, an employment benefit, a recruiting tool and a competitive advantage.

Dynamic Learning that Drives Success

Business owners are somewhat daunted by this idea of collaborative training and engaged learning, not because they dismiss the value, but because it is a departure from the way training is usually delivered. It requires their participation as a leaders, as owners of the process.

Training needs to be designed to foster culture and to align with strategy. In this way, the leadership must be involved. The fundamental purpose and continued success is tied heavily to the owner. This part of the process is often offloaded to human resources or outsourced completely, and ends up having no legs or real value. While these entities can certainly implement training and execute a program, the leaders of an organization must champion and live this training model. You must walk alongside employees as mentors, collaborators, co-conspirators, if you will. Leaders are confident about their ability to run their businesses—but not in their ability to run the people.

When a robust, learning program is launched as part of a Strategic Talent Management strategy, business leaders can influence the people to drive growth and success. And their people will evolve with the company as it grows because they are constantly being challenged and engaged as learners.

So, how do you change the training paradigm at your company? What does it take to break away from the typical, formal training you might be delivering and focus on a networked approach? Here are some foundation concepts to get you started.

Cultural Assimilation

You've done a lot of homework during the Recruiting and Selection processes to ensure that the people you hire are a cultural fit—that they will thrive in your environment and mesh with the team. During Onboarding, you integrate the new hire into your culture, and during Training this assimilation continues.

Deliver a powerful introduction to your company that includes your vision and mission. Tell your business success story. Get to the heart of what makes your company tick, what keeps you up at night. Paint the picture so they can imagine themselves in your culture, contributing and succeeding.

Ultimately, you want your people to make smart decisions for your business without constant and total oversight. You must trust them, but they need to know how your business thinks first, and what matters. When employees understand the company vision, they can function better without guidance.

Set the Tone

Create a positive learning environment that builds employees' confidence and excites them about their futures at your organization. Allow for mistakes and give employees some leeway to learn by trial and error, experiment a bit (in a productive way). Reward achievements and encourage questions.

Expanding the Model

You need three types of insightful individuals to form a mentorship-advisory sounding board: a mentor, advisor and coach. A mentor is someone you look up to—someone from inside or outside of the organization who shares their experiences so you can connect that learning to your own development. Mentors translate their personal and professional experiences into knowledge that you can apply to your situation.

An adviser is someone within the organization who understands the internal landscape and can provide insight on how to navigate and manage that landscape, whether it be gaining industry, competitive or best practices knowledge.

A coach is also someone from outside of the company who sees the good, bad and ugly in you and can provide honest feedback, and who helps you tap your potential by challenging you to think differently, not with judgment or criticism.

Continuous Learning

Training can go beyond serving as an introduction or orientation to the company, or simply a skills-based curriculum. A robust training program will include those components, but more importantly plants the seeds for ongoing learning.

In today's fast-paced business environment, the learning never stops so we can continue to stay current, adapt new skills, gain fresh perspectives and understand the dynamic world around us. One example is virtual think tanks within companies—creative pods where employees can gather to discuss ideas and percolate over possibilities. A company may set aside a creative room, or set up calls where employees can dial in and share dialogue. Technology is forwarding the way we initiate continuous learning in the business environment. A bigger vision of training inspires curiosity, gives visibility, permeates silos and flattens hierarchies.

Cross-Training

We want our people to be flexible, and to develop skills and experiences so their talents can be leveraged across the organization. This goes back to Recruiting and our discussion about hiring for a job rather than thinking long-term about candidates' potential and how they might evolve as your company grows and matures. Cross-training is important for sparking creativity and collaboration: When we understand the roles our position impacts, we can design better solutions and work in concert to deliver more value. Cross-training will give employees the confidence to take initiative. You want to hire individuals who can be cross-trained so you can deploy that talent.

Talent Insight:

Consider your training methods. How are you facilitating learning at your organization? Show your people the power of accountability. By giving them accountability, you are giving them ownership.

Performance Management: Developing the Individual

As an owner or leader, you have the responsibility and obligation to provide candid, constructive feedback to the people who work for you. It is your job—it's an expectation of your role that you must take as seriously as reviewing your financials. It is also your privilege. Thoughtfully evaluating the performance of your people is mission critical to your company's success because your people ultimately drive your organization's growth and profitability.

Only a handful of people over the course of your life have the formal role or opportunity to tell you something about yourself that could make you better. As an owner, you do have that responsibility and privilege to give this feedback to your people. As a leader, your words matter. Your direction matters. Your insights and observations of employees' performance matters to the future of your company, and to each person you touch. You can make a difference in their personal and professional lives; you can help people improve. And not living up to this responsibility is often interpreted as not caring.

Training is the ready-made stage for fostering a collaborative culture and developing leaders to measure and coach the performance of their people. Ultimately, training is the arena for teaching and inspiring, and it directs what results the company will get from individuals. During training, you're asking people to internalize learning, to absorb a new concept, model or theory. If employees value an interactive, individualized and engaging training experience—and, indeed, the people you want working for you should value these cultural criteria—then the Performance Management process should challenge them to succeed. It will support them when they fall or confront difficult situations, and reward them for achieving goals and objectives. Performance Management should involve feedback specific to the job, role and relationships. Executed this way, it leaves no place for low performers to hide and creates fertile ground for growth.

Performance Management is interactive, a continuous conversation—alive! It is a conversation, meaning employees and managers are contributing equally to setting goals, measuring performance against objectives and talking about the future. Indeed, it's a valuable one.

Assess Performance with Confidence and Competence

When was the last time you sat with your managers for an honest discussion about performance evaluations? Are there guidelines in place? Is there a dictionary, albeit informal, that helps managers find the action words and understand what their words mean when they say to an employee: "You need to be more strategic," or, "You need to focus more on problem-solving?" And, how often is the feedback employees receive tied with an action plan—solid, direct insight on how to improve on areas that are deficient or could simply use some tuning up? In so many organizations, there is very little guidance for managers on how to measure performance—how to do Performance Management.

Most managers are not properly prepared for how to deliver performance reviews and what the ratings mean. This results in inconsistency, missed opportunities, frustrated employees, apathy toward the performance review process, and disinterest in moving forward personally or lending one's talents to propel the organization forward.

The biggest problem is not having the conversation at all, and what I mean is not initiating the performance review in the first place, and/or not having the tough talk with an employee about his or her failure to meet performance objectives. It's a huge problem.

Managers fail to talk about performance because it's uncomfortable. They may lack the tools, the words, and/or confidence to initiate and continue the conversation, or they simply do not want to initiate it.

They fear the feedback will be misunderstood by their direct reports, creating a tension that will be hard to recover from. They worry feedback will demotivate people and make matters worse. Or, they fear prior managers have rubber-stamped performance, so their great attention to the real development needs of direct reports will be hard to reconcile.

Managers worry about upsetting employees, spreading malaise to higher-ups or infecting the culture with a negative attitude. Maybe they are confident about delivering thoughtful feedback but have no advice or tools to offer, diminishing its value and causing the leader to feel useless.

Bottom line: They only see bad results from the process and miss opportunities to improve the organization. No one wants to be the bad guy. It's easier to avoid a potentially challenging discussion than to get into the heat of it and realize that you're stuck in a bad place. But, an easy side step in the short-run, could create a journey of a thousand steps to get back on track. Low performance of any kind is indicative of poor Performance Management.

Again, I emphasize: *The quality of Performance Management depends on the quality of the conversation.* It is NOT about the forms, or even the formality.

What needs to happen is a synching exercise where the owner/key leaders and managers sit down and talk about what Performance Management means, and clarify what their respective responsibilities are in this process. Remember, as an owner, you are obligated and privileged to deliver fair assessments that will help individuals improve. Doing this well has a direct impact on your bottom line.

First, managers must value their contributions to the process. The purpose of the conversation isn't to be mean or scolding, or to enforce one's own agenda. The goal is to share observations based on stated goals and measurable objectives, as well as the individual's performance from a subject, intuitive, fundamental and experiential standpoint. Managers must value their ability to evaluate: It is their job, their responsibility. It is their right to help direct reports reach their potential.

Ingraining this message into your leadership is so critical to effective Performance Management. Each manager owns part of this process as an evaluator. The information managers gather and the scorecards they generate for employees become the centerpiece of enterprise-wide talent discussions. A company builds its bench strength based on its ability to leverage talent—and this is only possible when an owner knows what talent exists. Managers deliver this information via performance appraisals, which ultimately unfold into a company talent inventory.

A Shared Language

Many organizations do not set or communicate clear goals and objectives for their employees in the first place. Then the performance review becomes a generic and meaningless assessment based on one manager's ideas— there's no common language among leaders. Leaders need a shared language to discuss talent. So, with a half-hearted performance review, no clear goals and little direction, employees become apathetic or disengage completely. The opportunity to build a trusting, collaborative relationship across the team is basically lost in translation.

Performance Management in the Strategic Talent Management continuum emphasizes the value of the conversation: the responsibility and privilege of the owner/leaders to provide honest, clear direction. And the importance of implementing a Performance Management infrastructure so everyone in the company recognizes how goals, ratings and rewards are realized. (We'll deep dive into Talent Inventory as a critical tool on page 141, where we address succession and employee engagement for business continuity.)

There is significant payoff for companies that invest in Performance Management. When Harvard University's John Kotter and James Heskett reviewed more than 200 companies for their book *Corporate Culture and Performance*, they found organizations with high-performance cultures perform three to five times better financially than their peers.

These organizations are having in-depth talks with employees about their performance and providing tools for improvement. But what's important for business owners to understand is, managers will not initiate these tough discussions with employees if they do not have the tools to provide them with solutions for improvement.

Managers avoid conversations about poor performance because they fear conflict. They worry that the critique will hurt the relationship; the employee will become demotivated, de-incentivized or even passive aggressive. They think, "Is this conversation, really worth it?" Some fear conflict, which is a performance issue in itself for that manager. Some avoid the conversation because offering critique without the tools to help someone improve can, in fact, feel mean. To avoid the conflict, they'd rather dodge the responsibility—isn't that HR's job? In other words, they have a fear of not having advice to give. Add to that the fear of the employee's reaction, "What if this person becomes defensive?"

So, again, is the conversation worth it? The answer: Yes, absolutely it is worth it. But the conversation is only effective when the team of managers is using a common language, and when managers are provided with the training tools to give their employees solutions. Training is completely imbedded in the Performance Management process. It is the solution—the opportunity—that employees can be offered upon delivery of a performance appraisal.

Straight Talk

The conversation is the grease of Performance Management. The challenge is, managers have different ideas about what *average* and *excellent* performances are when they are not clearly directed by the owner with a defined scorecard. The quality of Performance Management depends on understanding the company's goals and objectives, rating system and rewards. This is a big communication job that falls on the owner to deliver the message.

To do this effectively, layers of information must be communicated to managers so they have the confidence and acumen to deliver an impactful performance appraisal.

Performance is often viewed as one dimensional: does the employee meet quantifiable goals? This is often defined related to activities listed on a job description or some assessment of the employee's ability to fulfill the technical or tactical applications of the job. This is important—it does not define performance alone. Performance must also measure the degree to which employees fulfill cultural expectations, including: attitude, emotional intelligence, professionalism and adherence to culture. These interpersonal dimensions are ignored, overlooked or neglected and become the cancer that is not curable.

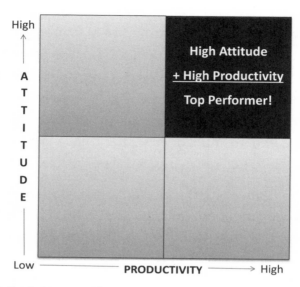

Figure 11: Performance objectives should be made up of two parts: productivity and attitude. Productivity can be measured using metrics and attitude can be measured using competencies. These two dimensions help frame the career conversation.

The Value of a Scorecard

Companies need a proper scorecard to understand the talent that exists in their organizations to leverage people and make the most of their assets. An often overlooked part of Performance Management is what happens after a manager's discussion with an employee about his or her strengths, weaknesses and areas to improve. What's often missing is the how. How does that employee think more strategically? What exactly should that person do to become a better leader, aside from joining a board?

Looking beyond the canned (repeated) suggestions, how does that person improve so they can rise in the company, achieve personal and professional success and be a greater asset to the organization? We forget the how or we tend to offer generic direction that feels more like a consolation prize to the employee for enduring the appraisal.

Rather than merely filling out a scorecard to rate an employee, let's activate it: Make that scorecard a launch pad for a potential fresh start for employees. Make it the ultimate conversation starter.

Name		Position	Business Unit
Current Manager		Prepared by:	Date

Objectives	Specific Examples of Performance	What supported or deterred the performance you expected?
1. Productivity objective		
2. Productivity objective		
Add more as needed		
1. Attitude/leadership competency		
2. Attitude/leadership competency		

Career Conversations:	Action Plan & Development Tools
1. What does it mean to you to be satisfied at work?	
2. What's the greatest value that you bring to your work?	
3. What are you passionate about that you're not pursuing?	
4. What about your work energizes you?	
5. What's the last thing you did to advance your career or improve yourself?	
6. What have been your greatest accomplishments?	
7. How can I support your career aspirations?	

Figure 12: A scorecard that activates employees toward future performance.

- *Performance scorecard*: This tool defines performance objectives and helps managers understand the metrics and behaviors that support an employee's ability to meet objectives. For example: ideal customer service means no mistakes in the ordering process—this is just one way to measure customer service.
- *Career conversations*: Inevitably asking career conversations lead you to ideas about current performance in a natural way, as well as provide insight into how people are feeling about their progress. There must be a common language.
  —What does it mean to you to be satisfied at work?
  —What's the greatest value that you bring to your work?
  —What are you passionate about that you're not pursuing?
  —What about your work energizes you?
  —What's the last thing you did to advance your career or improve yourself?
  —What have been your greatest accomplishments?
  —How can I support your career aspirations?
- *Feedback*: This is the direction and the observations shared with an employee about his/her performance. A common language is critical so managers can confidently and fairly assess employees. There are a number of books and competency models that provide details, and these resources should be utilized by the owner to establish a common language.
- *Incentives*: These are rewards for achieving objectives, and again, the measurements/metrics required to earn a reward must be consistent and understood among managers. Rather than applying bonuses across the board, implement performance measures that

offer incentives aside from money, such as: off-site experiences, sabbaticals, special projects, nominations for awards and publishing.

- *Total Rewards*: Provide a calculation of all the benefits provided, including training. Spell out the value so employees completely understand the investment you are making in their development and, ultimately, their ability to succeed and climb the ladder or increase their ability to contribute at your organization.

Performance Management at Work

We have emphasized the value of a conversation, and how an active, engaging Performance Management process can activate a culture and inspire innovative thinking. Here's how a Performance Management overhaul helped support a sweeping cultural shift at a large bank.

Talent Management, when properly linked to strategy, can move an organization forward in a profound way. A challenge for many organizations on this journey is that they tend to work in silos and might not consider how each Center of Excellence is interrelated—how they all work together to support an organization's strategy. It's easy to get bogged down in the details of implementing specific programs for recruiting or training. But with a holistic Talent Management perspective, you can completely evolve an entire organization. That's because change is about people.

Over the course of about five years, we implemented a sweeping cultural change at our bank. There are many chapters to this story, but I'll touch on some of the Performance Management activities we engaged in during our Talent Management journey—which is ongoing—and the power of transparency, setting clear goals and objectives, and defining leadership expectations.

Ultimately, we recognized that management team members who were resistant to change were serving as blockers to our strategic plan, which was to foster a culture of measured risk-taking and innovation. This strategy was a real departure from the way our bank historically operated, and the idea was unpalatable to some veteran managers, who approached the new strategy with a "this too shall pass" air of dismissal. This "new way" would fade, and they could continue their status quo method of managing in what had been a conservative organization that, arguably, stifled creativity.

To drive forward with our strategic plan, our people had to align with new goals and objectives. We needed leaders to think differently, to act differently. Most importantly, we needed to clearly define expectations so we could measure their performance and either coach, support them toward success—or make some tough decisions to drop the dead weight.

Through the Performance Management process, along with training and objective setting, we further clarified expectations, deliverables and outcomes. We held our people to those deliverables. We gave them support and time to improve. Some employees blossomed and emerged energized, engaged and became informal leaders within our group. They appreciated the level of clarity around expectations, and the empowerment that came along with personal accountability. Others could or chose not to adapt.

The key performance measures we set for our managers were:

- An ability to develop, support and coach their teams.
- Achievement at supporting the organization and, in particular, my team's direction.
- The clear, transparent communication of the change message to their teams.

Managers met regularly to receive extra coaching and support so they could better engage and develop their teams. They expressed their concerns and discussed what success should look like. Through coaching, they navigated the politics and began building trust among the team.

What resulted was a cohesive, unified team of managers with clear expectations about their roles, and our organization's goals. They understood exactly how they were being measured, and how they should evaluate the performance of their team members. There was complete consistency in the message, always. We discussed where we want to go and the competencies required to get there.

What we learned from this process: those performance measures, goals and objectives, give an organization the "sticky" power to incite change.

Talent Insight:

Focus on substance in your Performance Management efforts—substance trumps form. Have the courage to assume the serious responsibility of providing candid, constructive feedback to your people. They deserve it. Your company deserves it.

Leadership Development: Building Layers of Talent

Who is in the talent pipeline at your company? Who are your top performers next in line for key positions? Do you have at least two or three employees slated for each leadership position who have the attitude, aptitude and interest in expanding their contribution to your organization? In Recruiting, we learned about 70/30 rule of promoting from within vs. hiring outside talent. But the question you have to wrestle with is: if 70 percent of positions should ideally be filled with people who currently exist in the business, is that 70 percent being developed for a greater role?

Beyond developing individuals through Performance Management, Leadership Development addresses a more deliberate and selective investment in performance and people made by the company. The purpose of Leadership Development is to develop high performers and improve productivity—to fund the future of your company by committing the time to personally coach and develop the most promising contributors—your people. The purpose of Leadership Development is to facilitate promotions and ensure that a company has ready talent to "backfill" and secure critical positions in your company. It also ensures that the employees you identified as high performers, with a high adherence to culture—your ideal employees—are not a flight risk. Without an opportunity to climb and/or influence, these valuable individuals will leave.

When Leadership Development is properly executed in Strategic Talent Management, a company is constantly evaluating and identifying top performers and preparing them for promotion by providing new opportunities. In return, the company is less vulnerable and more likely to protect productivity when staffing or economic upsets occur. The organization becomes nimble, with the bench strength to take advantage of market opportunities that present growth opportunities for the business. And, the company becomes more innovative. Top performers commit more to the company because they are being nurtured and rewarded, challenged to create, invent and compete. Leaders look far beyond the scope of their jobs and add value in ways that drive production and become a competitive advantage.

Leadership Development should provide dynamic opportunities for leaders to test and challenge themselves— opportunities that are deliberately tied to the organization's strategic direction. Then, those top performers push themselves and the entire organization upward. Here's a case describing how this happens.

Brothers Carl, 52, and Travis, 48, co-owned a construction company that their father had purchased from the founder. The father ran it successfully until he died unexpectedly. Quickly, the brothers decided to leave their jobs to run the company. At the time, Carl was 32 and Travis was 28. They had their own careers and had started families. The brothers had never considered taking over the company. Yet suddenly, they had become co-owners of their father's company.

When the brothers took over the company, it was a $4-million firm. When they began developing their exit plan, it was a $17-million operation. Their plan was to own it for another ten years, when the company turned 100. Carl would then retire, which he was not really ready to do. While Travis would pursue a second career—the one he originally wanted.

The co-owners had no succession plan; no one was in line to assume ownership of the company. The three senior managers were reliable, capable and competent but not in a position to run the company. The company was incredibly vulnerable, and the family risked losing the value of their life's work.

Family businesses often fight through a complex web of circumstances when determining what's next for their companies when the owners are ready to exit. There is a legacy at stake: Should the owners preserve the business, or sell it? And, are the owners prepared to make that life-altering decision?

Transition planning was critical to give Carl and Travis choices. They needed to focus on building bench strength—thoughtfully and methodically—to develop their talent pool. This allowed them to explore options for transferring ownership, transitioning leadership and enhancing the business's value.

After a deep-dive look into the company and the owners' beliefs about what was possible, a real succession planning blocker was discovered. The brothers had a silent and unwritten agreement to never talk about work at home. They did not want to bring business concerns home to their families—they didn't want to involve their families at all. They felt obligated to take over their father's business when he died and pride in continuing his legacy, but they were strongly opposed to saddling their children with any such burden.

During the initial phase of this work, with the help of a coach and Strategic Talent Management mindset, the brothers: 1) Explored their reluctance to involve the next generation, and found they had an important story to pass on; 2) Discovered viable succession opportunities through an in-depth review of talent across the enterprise; and 3) Shaped a new vision for the company that included the next generation.

Ultimately, Carl and Travis were compelled to tell their story to their children. They agreed their college-bound children needed decent exposure to the company—if anything, so they could understand and appreciate the legacy. The brothers arranged a series of family retreats, which began by introducing their children to the company through a PowerPoint presentation and talked about the privilege of running their father's company, and why the next generation should have the opportunity, if they desired.

Carl's oldest son took a huge interest in the business and, fortunately, he had enough time left in college to refocus his studies. Travis's daughter began thinking about how her interest in business management and marketing could be useful in the business. The company had two potential family successors—and they began to prepare a next-generation integration plan with a curriculum, assessments and training opportunities.

Three-years later, the two oldest children wanted to work with their fathers and learn what it would take to run the operation. Carl was thrilled about staying on with the company for the duration of the transition to the next generation. Travis had options, which was what he felt he had lost years before when he joined the company. During the transition planning, the brothers assessed bench-strength, developed leadership and created a shared vision. As a result, the company continued in a way the brothers never thought possible.

Developing the Next In Line

If you are growing your business by 10% to 20% year over year, your top performers should be in new positions every three years, which means, every three years, you are expanding their roles and ability to contribute to decision-makers' dialogue. Maybe there isn't a formal title change, but those top performers are growing at an equal pace with your business—and you are filling in the ranks with the next generations ready to move up.

Many middle-market companies are growing at this 10% to 20% rate (or greater), but their talent gets stagnant. The same people fill the same roles. Maybe managers take on more work, or perhaps new employees are hired to assume different tasks. But rather than fostering a culture of learning, and challenging leaders to sharpen their skills and to think big, there's a stifling ceiling that keeps top performers from moving up with the company. This is usually unintentional. But it is damaging and results in turnover and, eventually, difficulties managing through transitions because the organization is constantly seeking and training new talent. You want to dedicate time developing talent, not finding it.

The case for Leadership Development is evident in research. Developmental Dimensions International conducted a study of clients across various industries regarding the bottom-line impact of leadership development systems. Twenty percent of respondents reported that positive changes were worth $500,000 to $1 million. Another 40% reported a return on investment between $50,000 and $200,000. Respondents said that more than half of positive changes were directly attributable to leadership programs, while 20% said that all of the changes were a direct result of Leadership Development.

Leadership Development brings significant value to organizations because it creates multiple levels of talent. As one layer moves up, another steps in, and still another prepares for launch. Leadership Development is building bench strength. Think about it: When a player on the field gets injured, there's another teammate ready to step in and take the team to a win. That's exactly what you want to be doing with the talent in your company.

But how? First, you'll identify leaders for specialized training. Then, identify leadership competencies and determine areas where top performers need to boost their skills and experience with authentic, strategically minded opportunities. Your Leadership Development program will be highly customized for each individual and the position they seek next.

Selecting Leaders for Specialized Training

Leadership Development requires an organization to invest in the individual. While Training is enterprise-wide, and Performance Management is one-on-one direction, the Leadership Development piece is the heart of coaching. It's when a company identifies top talent and makes the decision to invest in her or his rise up the ranks by providing meaningful learning opportunities. Remember, people should never wait for their company to select them for coaching in order to get coaching. Take your own initiative and determine yourself that you're worthy of getting your own coach.

Because Leadership Development is an investment, top performers must be thoughtfully selected for grooming. Performance Management tools, including a talent inventory and a history of performance appraisals, will shed light on the top talent in your company. Meanwhile, there are specific competencies that top performers have, which must be fine-tuned and/or enriched during coaching or through experiences provided by Leadership Development.

The attributes of a top performer are:

Maturity: An understanding of yourself within a larger context; to draw lessons from your own successes and failures; to facilitate the learning of others; to see the value of multiple perspectives; to respond in situations, not react to them.

Ambition: Competitive and driven, a desire to out-perform by putting out effort towards achieving a higher level of performance than before. This includes having accomplishments and experiences where success was achieved by overcoming obstacles and barriers, and where failed situations serve as fuel to try again.

Curiosity: A desire to learn and grow; to seek the root cause; to grapple with ideas and look beyond the obvious; to learn on the fly and bring intellectual horsepower to explore new concepts.

Self-awareness: Perhaps the greatest competitive advantage—the capacity to be outside of oneself and to look in; to see the world and how one's talents fit into that scope; to self-correct; to embrace your immense capacity for growth; to use yourself as a reference point for greatness; to be unencumbered by other people's standards of excellence; and to reach inward for the energy to improve and enhance your own circumstance.

Leadership Development At Work

Giving top performers experiences to grow their thinking and collaborate with other leaders shows them possibilities for expansion and development. Here is how the bank we introduced earlier continued its Performance Management initiatives with some grassroots Leadership Development programs that are helping managers learn and collaborate.

Sometimes, people need to be awakened and given permission to rise to the occasion. For me, a big part of Leadership Development has been stepping back and thinking broader about how I connect with my team, and how my team connects with each other and me.

Speaking to that, we launched several initiatives to improve career planning and talent development. One of those is a supervisor/manager forum that becomes dedicated coaching time. These top performers pick a topic that they want to learn more about. We may bring in an outside professional to talk about the topic, or ask a manager from another department to kick-start the topic. Then, there is open dialogue and time to discuss experiences and best practices.

This forum has accomplished several objectives. For one, it has helped bring together disparate functions in the organization so key personnel can view one another as teammates working toward a common goal. Also, it has fostered a new collaboration that is critical for implementing strategy—and, in particular, a sweeping cultural change.

From the forum, a safe zone emerged where leaders could ask each other questions and seek advice without going directly to their own superiors. The forum is building leadership competencies. I do attend these meetings, but as an observer. I sit on my hands and let them talk. I listen and learn from the conversations.

Aside from this initiative, we also started an employee-shadowing program where employees can rotate to different jobs to build skillsets. This helps them get to know other areas of the business. From this, we will build out a more robust training program.

These initiatives have shown our performers the possibilities to grow in our organization. Today, there is an excitement in employees' voices and an energy we did not see before. There is hope instilled, and I have seen some demonstrated examples of taking measured risk and innovating where that was not happening before in our culture.

Give Leaders Authentic Opportunities

Off-the-shelf Leadership Development programs tend to focus on behavior change—helping leaders act differently so they can fit in. This is not a sustainable model. Leadership Development should provide authentic, dynamic opportunities for top performers to challenge their skills— perhaps get a bit uncomfortable in the pursuit of personal and professional growth so people can contribute more.

Leadership Development is achieved with the guidance and support of a coach who brings an intimate understanding of talent management and rich experience in building bench strength. The old saying, "It's lonely at the top," is certainly true for many owners and C-level executives. Stop thinking this way. Why should you be alone during the climb, or while on the trek toward optimizing your personnel power?

Coaching is integral to the Leadership Development process because we need the foundation and beams from a practiced professional to rise up. Coaching is also critical to this Center of Excellence, and the entire Strategic Talent Management continuum, because the process requires such deep, personal reflection that we can't expect to do this in an honest fashion without some outside perspective. It requires a coach: someone who will rigorously challenge the status quo, provoke self-examination, and provide the business analysis tools to create a stronger, more sustainable culture that becomes a breeding ground for uncommon talent.

𝓣𝓪𝓵𝓮𝓷𝓽 𝓘𝓷𝓼𝓲𝓰𝓱𝓽:

Self-awareness is a leader's ultimate competitive advantage. Helping people evolve their mindset is the formula for getting people to contribute their best.

Corridor:
Deployment

In the Strategic Talent Management continuum, the Deployment Centers of Excellence (Talent Inventory, Succession, Employee Engagement) focus on building bench strength: backfilling key positions and creating a culture of employee engagement. Specifically, Talent Inventory provides tools for creating a talent slate and sparking meaningful conversation about the future; Succession addresses how businesses develop high performers to assume positions of leadership; and Employee Engagement is when employees take ownership over their roles and a relationship solidifies between company and individual, entity and community.

Talent Inventory:
Aligning the People

Agility is the ultimate competitive advantage of an organization. High-growth organizations with a deep bench of ready talent—valuable players lined up to fulfill key positions—are prepared to react swiftly and execute effectively. That's because there are no holes allowing wind to pass through the sails. When the right people are positioned in the right places, the correct roles, businesses realize the sweet spot of talent alignment. Their people are in jobs they were made to do. Their people's enthusiasm and drive penetrates the culture. They share a desire to win and propel the company toward its goals. When the A team is on the field, watch out! It's all about increasing value, improving efficiency, being productive, generating revenue. It's a winning formula for everyone.

Getting to this place, where your players are properly positioned to personally excel and professionally peak perform, is a journey. It begins with recruiting the right people, and selecting talent that suits your culture and speaks to the company you will be not just who you are today. It continues vibrantly and efficiently orienting them to your environment—Onboarding. Then you train them and collaborate with them to optimize their performance, and invest in them so they can develop. Next, we land on Talent Inventory on the Talent Management continuum. This is the process of assessing talent, creating a slate, holding honest discussions with managers during a process, and engineering a plan to ensure the people are strategically aligned. It's understanding the strengths and weaknesses of your players across the enterprise, getting that on paper, and determining a game plan for what's next for them.

Talent Inventory is a crucial precursor to succession planning. It's a tool to manage the performance and potential of people at all levels of the organization. And, the inventory gives the owner or CEO a clear map of the company's greatest asset: its human capital.

With that, an owner can leverage talent across the enterprise. A leader can tactically position team members— even upset the assumed route toward promotion by, say, shifting an operations manager into sales leadership, or vice-versa. The purpose of the Talent Inventory is to look at the current talent in a specific and individual way, then in a broad and global sense.

Talent Inventories include a few key components: 1) a facilitated meeting of peer group of managers; 2) a scorecard with narratives and examples of each leader's individual direct reports; 3) a common language for discussing employee performance; 4) a 3 x 3 grid for assigning talent; 5) an action plan for aligning talent to the succession plan.

Engaging in the Talent Inventory process is a brave step for the owner/CEO—it's a commitment to initiative challenging discussions and to make tough decisions. It's also incredibly empowering. In my practice, owners who initiate a Talent Inventory tell me a few things: For one, they'll never hold on to dead weight again, now that they know how underperforming individuals infect an organization and drag down top talent. They suck the life out of motivated performers. Owners tell me they now approach recruiting with clarity, with a strong grasp of the type of individuals they must hire to grow and realize goals. Leaders feel energized because they now have a visual representation of the human capital across the enterprise for aligning talent to create a smarter-working organization. The process produces a great number of epiphanies, to be sure.

So, how does a Talent Inventory scenario play out? Let's walk through the process following a company, Ready Corp., a fast-growing manufacturing firm with 48 employees, ten of whom have been with the company since it launched seven years ago. CEO Mark is at the helm. We'll walk through the Talent Inventory process using this company as an example.

Ready Corp. is a fictitious company. But its people scenario is based on of my work with middle-market businesses in a range of industries that are engaged in the Strategic Talent Management process.

Prepare to Take Inventory

There is a science to aligning talent: putting the right people in the right positions. There are tools for measuring a person's attitude and aptitude—we talked about those in Performance Management. But specific to the Talent Inventory process, there is a narrative managers will complete for each employee. The narrative is guided by a template that addresses an employee's performance and potential. A rating system is used to complete this form. I gravitate toward the check/check-plus method because it erases preconceived values associated with letter and number grades. So, there's the scorecard and managers describe performance in paragraph form for each direct report prior to engaging in the Talent Inventory session.

Of course, preceding this appraisal form is a meeting of explanation during which the owner/CEO lays out the purpose of conducting a Talent Inventory, the goals of the process, and each manager's responsibility as a stakeholder in the company's talent.

There are a few key messages to communicate to managers prior to launching the appraisal form and beginning the Talent Inventory process. First, managers must understand that their judgment is a valued and crucial component to raising the talent at the organization.

Also, they should be reminded of the confidentiality of this process. What discussions are held in Talent Inventory sessions and revealed on are not to be revealed outside of that room, beyond that circle of leaders.

Additionally, key leaders engaged in the process must recognize the commitment of time and attention.

Finally, they must agree that they are fully committed to the process and to serving as a stakeholder (or stewards) of the company's talent. Their opinion matters—their evaluations shape promotions and tough decisions.

At the same time, the owner/CEO is doing some soul searching, reflecting on:
- How the company has evolved
- What challenges have been faced
- How people played into the ability to overcome or be stopped by obstacles

- Where the company is weak on the field
- What positions need fine-tuning or retraining or a new player altogether
- Who's in line behind the starting lineup in case of a trade (losing a valuable employee)
- The mission-critical positions in the company
- Who is filling those positions now
- How those individuals are performing against objectives

Ready Corp. had matured through the initial business stages. It shifted from an entrepreneurial start-up with a few key people and a single office into a profitable business with a headquarters, substantial market share, and three layers of talent (executive suite, managers, individual contributors). There's Mark, the CEO, followed by his executive team consisting of a controller, VP of director and VP of operations. Then, the firm employs three managers who steer company's key divisions and oversee the 41 direct reports who are Ready Corp.'s producers.

There's a lot of talent at Ready Corp. And, like most companies, there were plenty of weak links and individuals with promise who were stuck in positions that weren't quite right for them. None of this was realized until a Talent Inventory was created and launched.

Mark took some time to map out the key positions at Ready Corp. What roles absolutely could not be outsourced? He also considered which roles had experienced a great deal of attrition—some positions had revolving doors, with new hires placed in those spots every few years. (Why?) He made a list of people he considered loyal and in the game, his partners in growing Ready Corp. Some of those people had been with the company for a long time; others were relatively new on staff, but showed promise as potential directors as they developed their careers. Then, Mark plotted out the key positions and wrote the names of individuals currently holding those jobs. Basically, Mark played out the process he was going to ask his three managers to participate in during the Talent Inventory.

From there, he invited his three managers to engage in the Talent Inventory process—managers who would assess and rate their direct reports and participate in the discussion of each individual's performance and potential. He also chose a facilitator who had been advising him through the company's growth. Including Mark, which meant five leaders would be involved in the Talent Inventory session.

Mark laid out a few goals: 1) Identify under performers; 2) Identify high performers who represented the next generation of Ready Corp.; 3) Determine core employees and discuss how their talents could be leveraged; 4) Create a slate where, eventually, each key position could be backfilled by three personnel-in-waiting to ensure no talent gaps; and 5) Begin the succession planning process.

The Value of an Inventory

A Talent Inventory is critical to an organization's success because when implemented successfully, a company will never be at a loss for talent. The reason Mark engaged in the Talent Inventory—and why all leaders should implement this process—is for these key reasons.

First, a Talent Inventory allows leaders to identify talent and assess strengths and weaknesses across the enterprise. It provides a system for comparing employees apples-to-apples when considering promotions and job moves across the organization. It also promotes honest discussion about the company's most important asset: its people.

Next, a Talent Inventory gives the CEO/owner a tool to deploy talent. It serves as an assessment of the company's bench strength and a jumping off point for initiating strategies to better align talent. It also compels leaders to be more prepared, thorough and thoughtful about their views and evaluations of the people for whom they are responsible.

Finally, the Talent Inventory is a dynamic process where leaders peel back the layers of talent and organize personnel according to human capital needs. The inventory provides a measured, visual interpretation of who's who at the company. This tool is a starting point for discussions mapping performance and potential, and underlying these two dimensions is each employee's performance history relative to productivity and attitude.

Words Matter

One challenge with the Talent Inventory process is, again, the conversation. We talked about the importance of the conversation in Performance Management—the responsibility of owners/CEOs to provide constructive, earnest insight to employees. The same principle holds true in Talent Inventory: words matter. That is exactly why conducting a Talent Inventory is typically so daunting for many leaders. They simply do not feel equipped to talk deeply about their talent. The descriptors assigned to people in a performance appraisal, or an appraisal form specific to the Talent Inventory, are wildly subjective.

"Janet lacks attention to detail." Does Janet forget to finish a job? Does she ignore instructions? Are we saying she is an average performer?

"Bill needs to sharpen his leadership skills." Are we saying that Bill has trouble delegating? Does he need to be more strategic? Do we want Bill to gain more experience in leadership by managing a special project or by sitting on a board? Is this a way of saying that Bill is not going to be promoted, or that he is on the slate to move up once he can master some skills?

"Judy is a strong communicator." Does she gain buy-in? Or, does she instruct and evaluate well— but she tells people what they want to hear and avoids conflict? Perhaps she is charismatic, and the comment is not reflective of leadership at all. What does "strong" mean?

Managers' assessments of direct reports can vary widely depending on a leader's experience, which is often revealed by the words chosen. Leaders may place varying degrees of importance on the review. They may show different levels of empathy and maturity, competency to coach, leadership style and more.

A leadership dictionary filled with competencies defined in detail can help leaders narrow in on the specific aspects of performance a person does well or poorly. This expectation that words matter sets the bar high for managers who are providing feedback and for employees who are asked to do something with it. That way, a manager doesn't just choose the competency "action oriented," they also describe "enjoys working hard; takes action, brings energy for the things he/

she sees as challenging; not fearful of acting with a minimum of planning; welcomes challenges, can be relied on to accept new projects."

With specific words to describe performance, everyone at the Talent Inventory understands what aspects of action-oriented this leader is recognizing. Along those lines, if you choose to have a rating system, clear parameters must be set for the rating system associated with the appraisal form. What does a check mark mean? Can there be a check-plus? This is important for holding employees and managers accountable. What is the employee expected to do to improve? And, how will the manager support this improvement? This tone and direction comes directly from the top, which is why the CEO owns this process.

Now, as for actual Talent Inventory session, a facilitator—either a consultant or perhaps HR—will launch the discussions and the owner/CEO will listen, and interject when appropriate (but mostly listen).

With tools such as a leadership dictionary of competencies, and a key to the rating system, leaders can fully engage in the Talent Inventory process knowing they are speaking the same language and holding up the same bar. This will avoid confusion and create a level of comfort for holding honest discussions.

Taking Inventory: The 3 x 3 Talent Grid

A key instrument to aid in the discussion of talent across the enterprise is the 3 x 3 block tool. The box grid originated within McKinsey to assess different business units and to prioritize the investment in individuals.

The grid measures performance and potential. It has three horizontal and vertical columns for the ratings low, medium and high. The vertical axis is potential; horizontal is productivity. Performance is a combination of attitude and productivity (see example below).

The 3 x 3 is a straightforward tool for calibrating talent as a group, regardless of division or department. It facilitates dialogue among leaders, identifies individuals' development needs, leverages and deploys talent across the enterprise and initiating succession planning.

This visual illustration serves as a talent chessboard. Upon careful analysis and based on an overall strategy, pieces are moved on the board to ultimately secure a win.

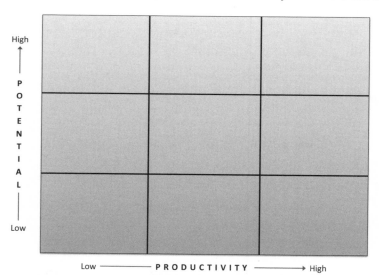

Figure 13: This 3 x 3 grid measures employee productivity against potential.

Here's how a company plays. First, the preparatory discussion and "rules" are explained to leaders—we just discussed those measures. Then, managers complete a scorecard on direct reports and bring those to the Talent Inventory session, during which a discussion is launched based on the criteria (a rating system, including competencies prioritized to describe performance).

While managers lead discussions about their own direct reports, everyone in the room is expected to weigh in with their interactions with the employees being discussed, along with their impressions and observations. The reason for this is employees have interactions with other departments, and the quality of their work and willingness to collaborate is viewed by people across the organization. Based on that discussion—and, indeed, it will be heated at times with some possible sparring over whether an employee is ready to take on a new role, or if he needs more time cross-training in his current role—employees are placed on the 3 x 3 grid.

What you get is different managers measuring the same group of employees—and varying opinions on an individual's performance and potential: where this person belongs on the 3 x 3 grid. This open discussion is the gem of Talent Inventory. During the facilitated conversation, employees are placed on the 3 x 3 based on their scores for performance and potential.

There are nine positions in the 3 x 3, as follows:

- *High Performer = Expansive Leader* has the highest potential, top talent, needs reward and recognition, promotion and development. Could be a flight risk if opportunities don't come available.
- *High Performer = High Impact* is a strong contributor who needs to be developed and motivated to grow. Has more to contribute and can take on more scope, has currency and credibility and likely can bring others along.

- *High Performer = Trusted Expert* is a specialist who has reached career potential, has depth of understanding, is relied on as a subject-matter expert, can reward and help develop others, and needs to impart knowledge to next generation leaders.
- *Core Performer = High Caliber* has potential to advance, is a valued talent and highly motivated, ambition can be ahead of readiness, and providing recognition and development is critical.
- *Core Performer = Vital Core* is motivated and engaged, a valuable player that should be rewarded, stretched with important work, willing to take risk to make the company better, collaborative team player.
- *Core Performer = Mastery* is a subject-matter expert who has reached career potential and needs further engagement broader scope of influence. Holds valuable institutional knowledge and can mentor others as a stretch assignment.
- *Low Performer = Dilemma* is an underperformer, who should be developed if in a new role, or it should be determined if individual is in wrong role or being led by the wrong manager. This "box" is a holding spot; it is temporary and requires immediate assessment.
- *Low Performer = Up or Out* is an underperformer, who should on their own volition kick it up a notch and prove their worth, or be let go.
- *Low Performer = Drain* has reached his or her job potential, shows no interest in advancement and lacks engagement/interest in coaching and should be let go.

Eighty percent of an organization's people fall into the Core Performer blocks, 10% are high performers, 10% are low performers. The hot spot of this 3 x 3 grid are the four, top-right blocks: High Performance/Expansive Leader; High Performance/High Impact; Core Performer/High Caliber; and Core Performer/Vital Core. Individuals in those blocks are your development priority.

	Low ———	PRODUCTIVITY ——→ High	
High ↑ P O T E N T I A L ↓ Low	**Dilemma** Underperforming but has not tapped potential to advance	**High Caliber** Consistently outperforms, elects challenging assignments, ambitious	**Expansive Leader** Top performer, vast potential, capacity for complexity, driven
	Up or Out Inconsistent performer. Unreliable and unpredictable	**Vital Core** Consistent, reliable, energized, progressive career development	**High Impact** Strong contributor, credible, influential and deliberate
	Drain Has reached job potential, and consistently under performs	**Mastery** Specialized, expert, technical talent. Reached career potential	**Trusted Expert** Influential, strategic vision, mentor

Low ——— **P R O D U C T I V I T Y** ——→ High

Figure 14: 3 x 3 highlighting the top-tier employees

Now, let's return to Ready Corp. to see how it used the 3 x 3 during a Talent Inventory, and what its results revealed, specifically in the *moving on* blocks (Low Performer/Mastery and Low Performer/Drain) and the *hot spot* of the 3 x 3.

First, Mark addressed low performers who were dragging down the organization. If his leadership team allowed this poor status quo, how could top performers be expected to stay onboard? Mark knew there were a handful of individuals who were infecting the culture because of their lack of desire and motivation—they just didn't care and didn't want to be coached.

135

The managers responsible for those individuals were coached on how to lead a discussion with their low performers. These employees were given the option to engage in a three-month action plan toward improvement; it was articulated that attitude and productivity mattered just as much to the company as it should to the individual.

Underperformers experience low job satisfaction, low motivation and risk missing their calling. People should be encouraged to find new opportunities that will engage them. Any more, it's not just about keeping your job or getting fired. It's about being productive, engaged and finding purpose in the work you do or the environment in which you work.

The Talent Inventory & Organizational Change

The agility gained through the Talent Inventory process is critical for implementing organizational change. During the inventory, owners/CEOs identify change-makers, champions, productive supporters and those who will resist change, or back away from it.

Initiatives for positive change can get stalled or derailed when people aren't engaged. But if business owners can assess their talent to identify those ambitious champions, and to separate out the stubborn, often subtle resistors, they can line up their army of people and assign them to the roles critical to achieve long-term objectives.

Change isn't hard; we're built for it. We venture into it on a regular basis. What we hate is changing habits to replace those habits with new behaviors. With a Talent Inventory, you gain an honest picture of who's who in your organization. That information can then be used to direct Performance Management and Training efforts—and more. The Talent Inventory becomes a key to your people, in a sense. Knowing what and with whom you are working—and having Strategic Talent Management in place—gives you the power to leverage your people. It makes you more agile. You can embrace opportunity, and change. You can grow and compete.

Interestingly, the Talent Inventory process often becomes a self-selecting process. Rather than dodging issues, accountability sets in. As one low performer was corrected and improvement attempted, this person decided the culture was not a fit for them—others who were in those low-performer blocks also exited. Meanwhile, the lift of burden was practically visible throughout the organization, especially among the vital core, some of whom were colleagues with low performers and frustrated about their apathy. At the same time, high performers were assured that Ready Corp. held standards for performance—that it didn't just hire and keep anyone. And this made the environment more desirable for climbers in the organization.

Immediately, the high-performer employees were identified and engaged for further career development to ensure their commitment to Ready Corp. These people represented the future leaders of the organization, and their value was expressed. The vital core was recognized and rewarded—and subsequently, Ready Corp. initiated more robust Performance Management and Leadership Development initiatives to provide greater growth opportunities for individuals. As the company began to accelerate, the team had to think on their feet and trust each other more. While titles don't always change, a growing company always pushes people to evolve in their role to perform at higher levels or more complex work.

Mark and his leadership team at Ready Corp. revisit the Talent Inventory on a semi-annual basis. They review the past 3 x 3, compare progress notes, introduce new employees to the grid (for appraisal and rating), and discuss how talent can be leveraged across the organization. Interestingly, one of Ready Corp.'s high-performing call center directors transitioned into an outside sales position. She had gained deep experience with Ready Corp.'s products, had a knack for communicating their benefits to customers and a real drive for her job. She is even more motivated by this career shift, and her depth of experience matched with her increasing breadth put her on the radar screen for succession planning and her fresh perspective becomes more valuable to Ready Corp.

Talent Inventories introduce surprises—good ones, like realizing that an empty VP of operations position could be filled with a highly motivated, vital core employee who's looking for an opportunity. The inventories introduce critical dialogue about people—conversations that are fundamental to building bench strength.

Talent Insight:

We have been sold a bill of goods about how people don't like change. In reality, people are built for change. We thrive on it. We wither without it. If people don't like anything, it's that they don't like to be told to change. People don't like being told by their company to "change immediately or else." People need to practice new ways of doing things. We require a learning curve, and a clear timeframe when trial and error is accepted and expected. Some will be early adopters, and they can be teachers to late adopters. That way, late adopters have some time to "catch on" without being mislabeled as resistant. Resistors in a well-thought-out process are often long-term low performers. The old fails because it misses the learning curve. Give the change a set time. As the owner, proclaim a trial-and-error period. Put the onus on you. After that time, shift accountability to the people. By then they'll be ready for it.

Succession:
Building Bench Strength

The business is not thriving, and the owner is not sure why. The sales team is hitting projections, and customers are happy—the client retention rate is above average. The company is growing at a steady 7% clip year over year. There's a gradual moving up, but no real energy driving the organization forward. Why?

The numbers and budget are in line. The production line is running efficiently, and the people who work at the business are satisfied. Business is chugging along, but still there seems to be a real lack of momentum, the owner observes. What could be wrong?

A question that most owners would never consider asking themselves relative to this scenario: What is the succession plan? What talent backup exists for key positions? How are managers training their successors? (Are they doing this at all?) And, when is the last time a top manager was promoted?

Succession is an uncomfortable subject for many business owners because it implies tragedy (a fatal accident, sickness, etc.), or some forced stop to running the business,

141

possibly retirement or a sale. Succession means, in the minds of many owners, "the end."

What many leaders are missing is that succession development is a valuable piece of Strategic Talent Management. Succession has become an urgent board issue with dollars devoted to making strategic decisions, while Recruiting is viewed as a cost center, staffed by entry-level employees.

Succession is not about planning the end—it's about calibrating people to launch new beginnings, to continue the lifecycle of the business. Succession is building bench strength across an organization, not for certain positions. Think big!

- Succession development is about identifying the next leaders, amplifying their commitment to the organization through Employee Engagement opportunities (our final Center of Excellence).
- Succession in Strategic Talent Management empowers these next-generation managers to keep the business alive, relevant, innovative, competitive.
- Succession pushes the organization full circle, back to Recruiting where their engagement draws in the best candidates for hire.

So, Succession is the beginning of…the beginning! If Succession is so valuable, then why aren't businesses engaging in the process? Here are some startling statistics— hard numbers that point out the insight I gather in meetings with business owners who simply don't do succession planning. They can't tell you why they don't engage in it, and they'll admit that it's on their radar. But succession is not an active process the company is working on as part of an overall Strategic Talent Management and strategic direction.

How prevalent is the lack of succession planning? Of middle-market business owners 55 years and older, 47% are interested in selling their businesses within three years. But more than 90 percent of surveyed business owners have not initiated the planning process, according to Bain Surveying Inc.

Succession goes beyond ensuring that there's a CEO in-waiting should the business owner exit. According to an Ernst & Young survey, 41% of respondents said middle management would be most affected by an aging workforce and a loss of experienced personnel. But, 75% of companies said they focus on succession planning only at the senior level.

Succession is all about development. It's means backfilling key positions at all levels of the organization, and ensuring that there are several individuals with the performance and potential to succeed if moved up in the organization. Succession is the point leaders should work up to during other Centers of Excellence, including Performance Management, Leadership Development and Talent Inventory. But, again, Succession is not the end. In fact, it is a critical component of any company's growth strategy.

Deeper than a 'Replacement' Plan

Why is succession planning so daunting to business owners that the process is avoided on a global level? First, consider the many meanings of the word "Succession" depending on who says it. When the insurance broker talks about succession, that conversation generally leads to life insurance policies, key person insurance, and buy-sell agreements. When an attorney broaches succession the discussion likely involves trust and estate planning. In family businesses, we are talking about preparing the next generation of the family to lead the company. When corporate America talks about the subject, they are talking about backfilling retiring C-suite executives. Succession with a Strategic Talent Management mindset is building bench strength. And, there isn't a policy you can buy or an off-the-shelf formula you can follow to accomplish building a strong bench of talent.

Succession in Talent Management is about developing a team that helps the company grow and thrive in the future, with or without the current owner/CEO at the helm. Succession is an enterprise-wide, human capital planning process with a risk management angle. By that, if a business owner neglects a succession plan, the cost is significant.

The benefit of succession was reported by international consulting firm, FTI Consulting, when it examined 263 CEO transitions at global public companies from 2007 to 2010. Compared with surprise resignations, planned CEO successions lead to a narrower range of stock price movement.

Planned successions do not guarantee a stock price bump, but they have reduced the potential for shares to fall off. Notably, McDonald's stock, after an initial drop off, increased from $88 to $103 a share during the nine months following the succession of CEO James A. Skinner by then president and COO Don Thompson.

Following Steve Jobs' resignation at Apple, the transition of CEO leadership to Timothy Cook did not hurt stock. In fact, it soared from $54 in August 2011 to over $100 in September 2012 ($114 in November 2014). These global corporations have been building bench strength for years, training and developing the next leaders, including Succession as part of an overall Talent Management strategy.

What's the Problem with Succession?

Here's why managers aren't doing succession development, and why businesses are not thriving as a result. (We'll share some good news, too—about what happens when succession is successfully executed, with our case study on pages 148–149.)

First, some managers hesitate to promote their high performers to the top because they do not want to shift core people out of their current roles. Who will replace the vital core? In some situations, an individual who deserves opportunity is held back because a manager is thriving because of this person's work. To raise this employee up and out of his or her role would mean a potential fail for the manager. Then, the manager would also take the risk of finding a replacement of equal quality. So, the manager avoids succession development and allows this high performer to stay in the role he or she occupies successfully. Why fix what isn't broken?

Meanwhile, a dilemma leaders face when developing talent to replace them is—well, what next for those leaders? Does that mean they are out of a job? In a well-executed, strategic succession-development initiative, the answer is an obvious "no." Engaging in succession means those leaders are also developed or their next moves in the organization, whether a vertical shift up or lateral move to a different division

145

with new, challenging opportunities. In an organization that operates with a Strategic Talent Management mindset, succession never means usurping a leader or replacing a manager. It's about lining up the backup players so when the entire enterprise is ready to act on an opportunity, its human capital is neatly aligned so the business can launch. In some cases people are inspired to perform better.

Another problem, managers are not taught how to develop their successors. Great leaders always prepare their successors—but that's scary for managers. What does preparation require? Who will help? (Who has the time?) By engaging in the Strategic Talent Management process, an organization organically develops a succession plan that can be solidified and fine-tuned. The reason is because the business is engaged in Training and Performance Management—identifying talent and raising up high performers. A Talent Inventory is in place so owners can refer to their slate of talent and act with agility. Beginning with Recruiting, individuals are hired into the company with the thought that they will progress beyond their initial job.

Implement Succession Development

The Talent Inventory is rigorous preparation for succession planning, giving owners a true picture of their entire organization. It gives managers a new language for talking about talent, a platform for assessing and placing talent on a slate, and a format for planning how to develop people and move them around in (or out of) the organization.

To launch the succession development process, business owners begin by reviewing the Talent Inventory slate and viewing people in terms of their attributes, readiness, attitude and potential—not what job they fill within a department. It's a cross-enterprise activity. Leaders must look beyond the job box and consider the character and winning qualities of their people.

Managers must be empowered to train their successors. This can be accomplished by initiating vibrant, relevant training programs that give people opportunities to challenge and prove themselves. The training of successors continues with Performance Management initiatives and Leadership Development. All of the Centers for Excellence leading up to Succession prepare managers to raise up their talent, so doing so never feels like a sudden burden placed on top of one's already demanding responsibilities. The training, the development is already happening. Managers, then, are charged with communicating with direct reports about career paths so their people see the vision and understand that they are working for more than a check-plus rating on their next performance appraisal.

Meanwhile, the succession plan or process should be shared at all levels of the organization so that individuals understand the fluidity of the company's structure: They're not stuck. They're going places if they display the performance and potential to rise and accept responsibilities and opportunities.

These conversations are empowering and energizing for companies. These discussions build morale and create loyal, engaged partners in a business's future. And that's exactly what a company needs to carry on into the future, where Employee Engagement is realized and the organization makes a great impact on its people and the community.

Case Study: Building a Legacy

Deborah is the managing director of a closely held, private family investment office, where succession is a complex issue because of the nature of the business. The office serves the second, third and beginning fourth generations of a family that, because of the cycle of life, is always in transition.

About 12 years ago, the chairman of the firm saw the need to make a change in the CEO/president role, and so he began collecting insight from management on what was working, and what was not. There were similar stories and themes emerging during those discussions; and the chairman ultimately decided the office needed a replacement president.

Deborah, who was head of tax at the time, said to the chairman, "Don't run out and hire someone else—we have lots of talent in-house that can do that job, and my experience in collaborating with other family offices, it's very difficult to bring someone in to manage the office effectively from the outside."

The chairman pulled Deborah in with a leadership coach to discuss the issue. After she made that statement, the coach—Stacy Feiner—looked at the chairman and said, "There you go. You've got your leader."'

Deborah was a fit for the operational complexities and customer service demands, and was promoted to COO. Her strengths were partnered with those of two technical investment experts with tenure. This team would co-manage the office. Deborah says, "I filled their gaps, and they filled mine."

Deborah continues, "Our office is filled with very smart, talented and technical professionals—but we know we have a drought when it comes to managers and supervisors and leaders in the organization. Stacy helped me work with the team and build a support for the organization. And, she led us through a talent identification exercise that aided in succession planning at the office."

What Deborah is referring to is a process of building an ideal candidate for a position by engaging a group of stakeholders in a discussion about the attributes this person must have to successfully fulfill the role. Participants fill out a questionnaire and responses are shared during a meeting. This profiling exercise provides businesses with a tool for talking about talent, matching ideal characteristics with what exists in the organization, and beginning to slot people into positions. It's the early framework of a succession plan, much like the Talent Inventory.

The goal is to spark critical thinking about what the ideal candidate for a position looks/acts/leads like. First, the hiring committee determines the core competencies for the following areas: functional skills, cultural fit, and future potential. Then candidates are assessed in those three areas, against the company's core competencies.

Employee Engagement: Fulfilling Aspirations

The world that you, the business owner, have to take care of is vast. No company can just account for the 200, more or less, employees who work for your organization. What about workers' spouses, children and loved ones—indirect stakeholders? That easily quadruples the business roster to 800 people. Then, think beyond those near-and-dear stakeholders and consider the entire community: customers, vendors, distributors, people who are affected by the goods produced and services provided by the company.

Leaders of an organization are stewarding a cause, not just a company. There are literally masses of people depending on a single business for some reason or another: financial stability, a career, maintaining their family's health, and more. That business must make a positive community impact, and in Strategic Talent Management, that is achieved through Employee Engagement.

In essence, Employee Engagement is the secret sauce of a company's culture. It defines a business in the community; it reels in talent and feeds Strategic Talent Management in the sense that where we end on the "circle"—Employee Engagement—is a critical building block for the very beginning, which is Recruiting. Indeed, the Strategic Talent Management process is a lifecycle, and leaders control the momentum.

Employee Engagement is a company's opportunity to create the ultimate competitive advantage. It goes back to the old sales mantra that people buy from other people they know and like. Consider a company with an entire staff of ambassadors—employees who truly care about the business, who are committed to its success, who take ownership in the business and personally want to see the entire enterprise reach goals. There's power in Employee Engagement, and that's why it is studied so readily.

But the results of many studies are quite disappointing because statistics reveal what so many companies are not doing to ignite this unified spirit—this desire to succeed as an individual and as an enterprise. Gallup's 2013 *State of the American Workplace* survey indicated that 70 percent of American workers are not engaged or are actively disengaged. They are emotionally disconnected from their workplaces and less likely to be productive. That lost productivity can cost the United States between $450 billion and $550 billion each year.

Now, let's take a look at the flip side: companies that fully engage their workforce, that have cultural core competencies in place and are activate in the community. Gallup says that companies in the top 25% of their engagement database have higher productivity and profitability ratings. So, organizations with an average nine engaged employees for every one actively disengaged employee experienced 147% higher earnings per share in 2010-11 compared to their competitors.

There are good, financial reasons to engage employees—and this doesn't just happen. A company absolutely must prioritize its culture and focus on executing Performance Management so individuals are fulfilled in their career aspirations and, therefore, realize the benefit of working toward the company's common goals.

Consider the national dialogue surrounding the trillions of dollars exchanging hands as baby boomers transition their companies to new ownership. Every transition is made better, and smoother, and is more rewarding and sustainable when the people within the company are engaged.

Rules of Engagement

Employee Engagement is a complex system involving the individual, stakeholders and the community. Each member of this family must have shared objectives that relate to the organization's core competencies, and these tenants essentially make up a company's mission and vision: who it is and what it strives to be.

If you think about a business as a person—indeed, it is a living, breathing, growing entity—and, culture to that company is like personality to a person. When the people are aligned with the company's culture—when they fit—they thrive. Effective Employee Engagement creates a culture where people can do their best work, and it should allow individuals to achieve their aspirations, and for the company to realize its goals. It is a relationship.

With the job-hopping behaviors of many individuals in the workforce today, Employee Engagement has never been more important. The average worker stays at his or her job for 4.4 years, according to data from the Bureau of Labor

Statistics. And the expected tenure of a workforce's youngest employees is about half that—less than three years. Clearly, the rules of engagement have changed.

But employees overwhelmingly want to work for organizations with values that match their own. A 2012 Net Impact survey found that 88% of workers prioritize a positive culture. They said it was essential to their dream job. And, 58% of respondents said they'd actually take a pay cut of 15% to work for an organization with like values.

All of this underscores the critical importance of building a positive company culture. Doing so benefits recruiting, retention, performance, profitability—and builds a company's bench strength. Employee Engagement is essential to Strategic Talent Management because it's the one outward piece of the continuum that takes all of the good work the company does internally and spreads that into the community by way of infusing a positive culture into people who pass it on.

Levels of Engagement

How does an organization activate its employees? By engaging them individually through Performance Management, and as a whole through cultural core competencies. First, a business owner must understand the various levels of engagement and how that commitment strengthens as an organization develops its Strategic Talent Management program.

The most basic level of Employee Engagement begins with Recruiting and then Training: setting expectations for job responsibilities. This includes protocols such as when the work day begins, policies and procedures, the information included in an employee handbook. This basic form of Employee Engagement is the welcome mat. A business is telling a new hire: here's what we expect of you. It's essentially a contract between the company and employee.

Taking that engagement to the next level, individuals are given clear objectives and tools to reach those goals. This process is covered thoroughly in Performance Management. At this level, the company and individual are mutually engaged in ensuring the success of both parties. They're in it together.

The sweet spot of Employee Engagement—perhaps the "platinum" level—is when the individual and organization share a symbiotic relationship where lines are blurred in terms of "this is for me" and "this is for you." At this stage, employees take ownership over their roles, their talents, their abilities as a stakeholder in the company to take their work into the community. They recognize that their work is a reflection of themselves, and of the entire organization. This is a Greater Good level of engagement—where an organization earns a competitive edge. This is the positive culture employees seek, the reason why a company can attract top talent.

Employee Engagement is a buzzword at corporations, and publicly held companies are well versed in the subject and most have processes in place to measure this aspect of Talent Management. Many middle-market businesses do not—and these businesses can supremely benefit from Employee Engagement because their people truly can feel a sense of ownership at all levels. And that is what "ultimate engagement" is all about. Also, Employee Engagement is critical for privately-held companies because the risk of not sending people out into the community with positive messaging is great. These businesses tend to operate closer to ground level—they're imbedded into the community. And, culture and engagement is critical for all organizations because generally their employees live in the community.

Establish Cultural Core Competencies

So what messages, exactly, are employees carrying into the community that reflect the business? And, how does a company build ownership into its workforce so that each employee is an authentic ambassador? The answer to these questions is in a business's culture core competencies—a set of tenants who define the culture. Think about this. Businesses have benchmarking and performance management tools, and talent inventories and appraisals to evaluate personnel. But how does an organization measure its employees' adherence to culture? This can only happen once culture is adequately defined.

The key conversation starts with leaders and a discussion about what the team expects of people who work there. Should all employees be independent, aggressive,

Are Your Employees Engaged?

It's a good idea to take a good, old-fashioned survey to find out. Here are some questions to consider, and be sure the format allows anonymity. You can use online survey tools to execute the company-wide survey, which will also compile findings and create some charts to use as discussion points in a leadership meeting.

1. Do you have clear objectives for your job?
2. Do you have the tools to accomplish your objectives?
3. Do you feel you have opportunities for career development?
4. Do you feel you are appreciated at work?

go-getters, technical, data-driven, resilient, etc.? What needs, from a character standpoint, must be filled in order for the company to be the "person" it wants to be? Here, we go back to the idea of culture as a company's personality. Before an organization can hire and train to the culture, it must precisely define what characteristics make up the company culture.

This sounds simple enough, but the process of diving deep and putting onto paper the company's *persona* can involve some tough conversations—and, of course, disagreements about what qualities are most important. But through it all, a theme will emerge. Common traits will be tossed into the ring and become the core qualities the organization wants to instill in its people. If employees do not naturally have those attitudes and aptitudes, they must be trained and developed to acquire them. This Employee Engagement exercise actively feeds Performance Management, and vice-versa.

So, what happens once a business nails down its cultural core competencies and actively trains and develops people to adhere to those values? That's when the individual and company begin to truly mesh into a powerful force— when employees take ownership and act as the company. When this happens, they take their company out into the communities where they live. Their mindset shifts from, "I'm going to work to do my job," to a feeling of living the work mission inside and outside the office building. And we're not talking about work-life balance issues here—rather, a sense of true spirit and desire to achieve and win as an individual and as a company.

Here's what companies should do right now to spark better Employee Engagement:

- **Survey the people**. Find out just how engaging the culture is right now so you can start where you are, whether that's at the basic level or more advanced.
- **Articulate the values**. Once core cultural competencies are nailed down, post them to the wall—literally. Shout them out over the cubicles; share them on the company's social media outlets. Tell employees and the world what the organization stands for…and why.
- **Take time to care**. A business that genuinely cares for its people—and shows it—will gain reciprocal attention from its workers.
- **Be honest**. Communicate often and in diverse ways. Establish an open-door culture where feedback is cherished and criticism is addressed. Everyone wants to be heard.
- **Provide career paths.** Show employees the opportunities that engagement will win them.

Talent Insight:

Business owners are knee deep with an underperforming workforce. They just can't get their arms around this elusive thing called talent. Most of their advisors can't either. After all they're the same people who refer to people as intangibles. The business owner's frustration is understandable because you can't oversee what you do not understand. But with Strategic Talent Management, owners gain understanding and, with that, control. They own the process. There's no giving up. There's exceeding expectations, wreaking havoc on the competition, and reaching dreams!

Launch Strategic Talent Management

When business owners master Strategic Talent Management, in a sense they're getting a master's degree in organizational development. It's a journey. Owners commit to the time and investment, and the tough conversations—they earn the wins that result.

You start where you are with Strategic Talent Management—where the pain is: recruiting, training, development, succession. Talent Management is a lifecycle, so there's no official starting line or ever any finish—the engagement is a commitment to work on people first.

Strategic Talent Management begins at ground level with soul searching about who gets invited into your company—because hiring, essentially, is an invitation—and it makes sense to know why each person is brought into the fold. You get real about the way those prospects are filtered and selected according to the organization's cultural core competencies. You reconsider the way those carefully chosen individuals are introduced to their jobs, and opportunities. You ask, "What's in it for the people? What's in it for the company?" Then, a realization: the People are the Company. And, given that, what asset could you possibly identify that means more to profitability, competitive edge and success? That's why Strategic Talent Management matters. A business's human capital is priceless.

But, there is an investment, and that's an equal consideration as business owners take on the supreme role of building their bench strength. How much? How much time, money, sweat? What's the input? What's the expected outcome? These are good questions.

Privately held, middle-market businesses might consider an investment of $150,000 in Strategic Talent Management per $1 million revenue annually. That sounds like a lot, doesn't it? Not when you weigh the investment against the current turnover rate and investment in training/onboarding a new hire.

For jobs earning less than $50,000 per year—which was more than 40% of American jobs in 2012 when the Center for American Progress report was released—the average cost of replacing an employee amounted to 20% of the person's annual salary (this survey looked at 22 corporate case studies). That's a $10,000 fee for every lost average worker. And that does not take into account the average 30% to 50% of the person's salary that employers spend onboarding a new employee.

Some studies say you'll spend that 30% to 50% to hire and unload a worker. This figure does not account for lost productivity cost to a business when a position is open in waiting, or when an inadequate worker is filling the job.

So, what's the tab for ignoring Strategic Talent Management? Better question: who can afford to ignore it? Not competitive, agile organizations that grow.

Ultimately, Talent Management is risk management for the people and growth platform. What company can afford to ignore its greatest asset? Considering today's highly competitive market places, what organization can afford to turn a blind eye toward the one competitive advantage companies have over any other? (Yes, the human capital.)

Ultimately, Strategic Talent Management is a catalyst for growth…The good news is when you address one the other falls into place.

But now comes the potentially daunting task of deciding where to start on this Talent Management journey. What does the landscape look like? Who will join the experience? And what's the agenda? Those questions can only be answered by the owner, who must steer this process and live it, breath it, believe it, and then instill it in individuals who work for the organization.

This book offers some thought-provoking material and infrastructure to launch a Strategic Talent Management initiative—but the process belongs to you, and you must customize it and mold it as if it were the very business that you created.

Strategic Talent Management is about returning to the blueprint, addressing the systems that affect the people, and establishing a construct that is uniquely designed to motivate, accelerate, invigorate and drive profitable success.

So, start where you are—and think big. You deserve a better product than off-the-shelf versions. You created a business—now shape your talent. Manage it like you do your numbers.

Understand Strategic Talent Management so you can assist human resources and course correct if necessary.

Once you learn the principles, you can apply those to your experiences—much like an owner with an MBA will apply those business course lessons to his or her own operation, personalizing the material to produce desired outcomes.

The Strategic Talent Management process is, indeed, a long-term commitment and perspective shift. It's a way of pressing the reset button on the way people have been recruited, trained, managed, developed and promoted. Is it time to press reset? Only you know the answer, and where to begin. Ultimately the Talent Management process belongs to you, the leader—you own it. You're the author and the hero of this story.

About the Author

Dr. Stacy Feiner is an executive coach for the middle market. Stacy brings psychological strategies to business owners to help them improve their performance, advance their organizations, and achieve the success they want and deserve.

Stacy's methodology addresses complex dynamics within owner-operated companies, family businesses, management teams and boards, and solves people problems that clear the way for driving strategy, growing profitability and eventually transitioning to the next generation.

Stacy is a licensed psychologist. She earned her doctorate in clinical psychology from the Illinois School for Professional Psychology, an MS from Northeastern University and BA from Hobart & William Smith Colleges. Stacy is a coach, author and national speaker.

Email Stacy at: stacy@stacyfeiner.com

Learn more about Stacy at: www.stacyfeiner.com